MUSINGS
OF A
Spiritual
HANDYMAN

TIM
DUNKIN

DunkinWorks
San Jose, California

The author of this book does not dispense medical advice or prescribe the use of any technique as a form of treatment for physical or medical problems without the advice of a physician, either directly or indirectly. The intent of the author is only to offer information of a general nature to help you in your quest for emotional and spiritual well-being. In the event you use any of the information in this book for yourself, which is your constitutional right, the author and the publisher assume no responsibility for your actions.

ISBN-13: 978-0-9795747-0-2
ISBN-10: 0-9795747-0-6

LCCN: 2007904365

Printed in the United States of America
Cover and interior design by www.KareenRoss.com

Cover photography by Brian A. Klimoski (www.pbase.com/brianowski)
Comments from Brian Klimoski regarding the cover image:
"Verdant green is not a color one often sees in Sedona, but after a moist Spring, the desert comes alive and brings to Sedona the perfect color complement to the red rocks.

On this evening, I marveled at how the desert had been transformed since the last time I was there. Flowers were everywhere; the grass was thick and green. Everything was humming with life and new growth. High cirrus clouds filtered the usual, brilliant red sunset colors this evening, softening the scene to reflect the muted feeling of the day. This image was composed to bring together these elements."

Dedicated to my friend, mentor
and father
Gene Dunkin

And to Jill Dunkin
Without whom this book would not exist

table of contents

preamble   7

beginning the journey   11

the order of things: cosmic/human/self   15

mega/mini choices/anchors   23

many paths to the summit   33

truth about angels   43

intent/thought/word/deed/reflection   49

karma: instant and otherwise   63

love, energy and light   71

learning vs. integration   79

teachers come in all forms   85

right choices/livelihood/life style/balance   91

balance: ebb/flow, consistency/centeredness,
product/process   99

developing the observer   107

humor/laughter/perspective   117

comparative mind/be here now   123

discipline revisited   129

living a God-centered life   137

reminders   143

about the author   147

preamble

Musings of a Spiritual Handyman is the next evolutionary step in my personal spiritual journey. I believe that each of us is in the midst of a journey, minimally a journey of living a life initiated at birth and ending with death. How we view this journey, what we believe came before and what comes after, and how we are to conduct ourselves along the way are the topics of thoughtful individuals throughout time. I consider myself such an individual.

I've had what seems to me to be a normal diversity of experiences, picked up degrees in philosophy and religion, became an ordained minister and left the active ministry, worked in the public sector and for non-profits, have read as many books as possible and talked with as many people as possible. Along the way, it became clear to me that the most constant and distinguishing characteristic of my life journey is its spiritual nature. In my discussions with different people, I'm at times more educated or well-read on a topic, and equally less educated or well-read.

I realized that I was interested in grasping the various concepts that caught my attention, and then attempting to apply them to my life and the world around me. I didn't feel a need to become an expert. I am quite happy that experts abound and have the ability to share their expertise with me and other people. That lets me off the hook! I can benefit from their dedication without paying the same price of discipline that they undertook. I can continue my journey.

My wife tells me that she appreciates the fact that I am handy. In fact, she says it is a definite asset. I'm able to paint the house as needed, fix small plumbing problems, dip into electrical issues, do all the yard work and build lots of things out of wood. I'm the old style handyman - jack of all trades, master of none. I know enough to apply my knowledge effectively, and call for help immediately!

The same is true for me relative to the world of spirit. I know more than most and am able to be an effective life coach to many, drawing upon the disciplines of theology, education and counseling. I am not an expert. I read and study the works of experts in all these fields. I do attempt to apply what I read, contemplate and experience. So, I view myself as a "spiritual handyman." I know enough to carry my end of a conversation, understand that the world is always larger than we think it is, and even assist another traveler on occasion.

Musings is the first of three books from the perspective of a *Spiritual Handyman*. Imagine sitting around the breakfast table or an evening's fire, and engaging with a friend about some life-based question. It would be an easy conversation, just a few folks sharing their ideas, telling some stories and adding as much humor as possible. *Musings* is that conversation. It is not a lecture or a paper to be published in the halls of academia, it is not a "how-to" book. It is simply musings. Hopefully, it will remind you of conversations you've had or would like to have. Perhaps it will spark an idea or make a couple of dots connect in a way that didn't before, or simply allow you to realize that there are truly different ways of looking at this journey we call life.

The other two *Spiritual Handyman* books will be more traditional in format, and will explore some of the ideas presented in this book in more detail. One will focus on the conceptual framework presented in this book, looking at the ontological perspective with both a historical and current eye. The other will focus on more detailed discussions of the applications suggested in *Musings*. This will provide more exercises, how to incorporate mind-sets and practical case stories that should assist one in developing a more focused spiritual life within this culture.

Be sure to check out the readings list at the back of the book. It is certainly not intended to be inclusive, though you might enjoy the range of authors and topics that have influenced me on my journey. Authors and their books have been my primary teachers, whether that is ancient scripture, modern literature, science fiction or comic books. If you are open, there are teachers lurking everywhere!

beginning the journey

How is life organized?
What is my place in the universe?
Do I have a soul? Does my soul have me?
What is living a good life?
How do I know if I'm doing it?
What is the nature of God? How do I relate to God?

Have you ever asked yourself questions similar to these? Where did you go to find answers? Were you satisfied with the answers?

These questions are common to many of us, and they become critical to individuals who feel it is time to begin a journey. We generally don't know it at the time - that we are beginning a journey, or the nature of that journey. It is a journey, a spiritual journey. It can happen at any point in your life and in any setting. You may be a person who attends the services of a particular religion, or you may see yourself as being completely non-religious. The call of the spirit is the soul reminding us of our primary purpose in life.

See? Words like "soul" immediately enter the conversation. What is this "soul?" Do you have one? If so, where does it show on the x-rays?

This book discusses these kinds of questions and provide some insights into the nature of the spiritual journey that many of us are called to focus upon during this life. I've written it in a dialog kind of style, as if we're hanging out around the kitchen table and you've just asked me, "Tim, how is it you are the way you are?" And I attempt to provide you with an answer. In fact, I've been asked just that question a fair number of times, and as I've worked on providing some comments, they've generated a fair range of responses. Some people are offended for the thoughts are too different from their own, some suspect the sixties were too good to me (not true), and some find the insights useful. So, this book is for those in search of answers or different ways at looking at this process we call life.

Be warned that I deliberately use words like "dance" and "play" and "melodrama" to talk about events in our lives that are very important and typically dramatic and potentially extremely serious. That's because we need to be reminded of who we really are, and to maintain some perspective. I'm in the camp that says, "we are a spiritual being in a physical body rather than a body that has a spirit." The order is critical to one's perspective. And if we cannot discover sufficient perspective, the dark side of life can simply become over-whelming.

I believe there is hope and joy in life. Sometimes we need some assistance in discovering that dynamic. We certainly are confounded with an abundance of information, and the "overload light" comes on with great regularity. There are so many books, articles, plays, shows, movies, emails and phone calls, all demanding our undivided attention. Just what should we focus on? What is the ultimate meaning that should be a part of regular reflection and consideration? The answers to these questions are found along the way of the spiritual journey.

As you'll discover, I strongly believe there is not one proper spiritual journey that negates all others. The good news is that the billions of people playing on this planet have a billion options from which to choose. The bad news is we have to choose. We have to consider "stuff" and make decisions. The tooth fairy is out of business!

I invite you to "muse" your way through this book. Feel free to read it in sections or from beginning to end. Read a bit, put it down, pick it up, share it with a friend, discuss it, weigh it and come to your own conclusions. Find your truths, and if someone should ask you, be willing to share. Enjoy.

the order of things:
cosmic/human/self

How is the universe organized? Is it organized?
Is there a God? Who or what is God?

Common questions to those entering the journey, so my base line answer is:

No one knows.

There is a vast array of theories, explanations and opinions. Wars have been fought and religions founded upon the true nature of God, the name of the Supreme Deity, the lack of a Supreme Deity, the order of the universe and our place within it. But no one *knows*.

Our knowledge continues to expand. We have traveled in space, and are currently building a structure in space. We've been to the moon, and we've sent scientific toys out to explore Mars and other dimensions of our solar system. We've taken really cool pictures via the Hubble telescope. We're being forced into a new perspective of Earth and its sun, the solar system and the vast nature of the universe. We're gaining new clues as to how it operates, and it forces us to reexamine our definition of life and self. But we don't *know*.

From a spiritual perspective, *we don't* know *either*.

In the face of not knowing, we generate beliefs, and these beliefs reflect our perspective within a particular space and time, which is to say, a refection of a specific culture and a specific time in history. If one is to review the history of the human species, there is an ongoing evolution of beliefs about how things are organized.

These beliefs are powerful. We do not treat them lightly, for they typically form the basis upon which we organize our societies, cultures, communities and individual lives. But if anyone claims they have the absolute truth about the nature of the life dance, I will have to pass. No one truly knows, most believe. And the beliefs become truths, and tremendous energy is expended in "proving" the "truths."

I'm not attempting to suggest that the cosmos is not real, does not exist, and is not evolving or that it is an illusion that we are supporting through some trick of the collective conscious. It certainly appears real to me, and each piece of evidence that we gather convinces me that it is incredibly vast, seriously older, wider, and far beyond my limited comprehension.

So how did it start? Is there a creator? Will it end?

Some argue it is our ability to ask such questions that sets us apart from other species of life. One might ask if it is an ability or a curse. But we do ask, and if we are honest, we must notice that we, in fact, answer our own questions. "The Gods have spoken." And that would be through whom? If we take a step back, the process becomes clear. We, as self-conscious human beings, become aware of a mystery in our lives, and want to know why, how, when, who. Not being satisfied, or able, to live with mysteries, we generate answers. These answers will consistently mirror our collective and cultural understanding of the universe for that time and place.

Being raised in the West, allow me to talk about God. God, in the singular, has been a key player for the past three to five thousand years. In the early ages, God had competition, but for the last two thousand years, there haven't been any major challengers that were not quickly swept aside. Now, for instance, if the American Indians had been able to hold the continent against the European invasion, perhaps this would be a different discussion. But God prevailed. The God of the West, known by several names – Yahweh, Abba, God, Allah, has a connected and evolving history, based upon interpretations of his intent, cultural expression and the general evolution of knowledge. The consistency has been in a male, theistic deity.

I argue that it is time for God to be updated again. It is time to let the theistic model go and move to a more appropriate model for our time, our knowledge and our understanding of the universe. It is difficult for most of us to rationally believe that there is a kingdom, ruled by God, that exists in literal space just beyond our atmosphere; that the stars are peepholes of light shining upon us from that kingdom, and God sits upon an actual throne observing us, judging us and occasionally directly intervening in our lives as his primary activities. Please understand, at the time of the writings of the ancient scriptures of the Judeo-Christian heritage, the brief description above was the prevalent understanding of the cosmos. That was reality, not a metaphor.

I was raised in the Methodist tradition, a sect of the Protestant branch of Christianity. I was raised to somehow believe the words to be true as stated, and yet accept them as metaphor when the current reality didn't match well. Being a believer, I could do this – for a while, at least. Somewhere during Junior High School, it didn't work for me anymore. So, I switched to all metaphor, but the exercise of constant translation became too tiring sometime after graduate school. As a quick example, think of the major events of the Christian story such as Christmas and Easter. They are wonderful stories that reflect the life of a very special person, but they are not literal history. For both stories, they are not consistent in either the actual Biblical references or the historical traditions. If you read carefully, you will find that there is no basis for camels, no stable and therefore no sheep, cows or donkeys at the stable, and no innkeeper. Mary was called a Virgin, she wasn't (all virgin birth stories ended when human knowledge figured out that women contributed half the genes to the new life form, and wasn't simply the vessel to hold the male sperm). And though I'm sorry to disappoint Mel, his understanding of the passion of Christ is based more upon his Roman Catholic traditions than an accurate Biblical basis. What I realized is that energy spent in constantly translating, separating fact from fiction, and dealing with individuals frightened by any challenge to their "truths" was energy not spent on more appropriate spiritual development and human assistance in real time.

So what are the answers? How did it start? Is there a creator? What is the nature of God?

Our God needs to be reflective of our current knowledge of the universe, which we don't fully understand and do recognize to be very complex and almost incomprehensible. We do need a non-theistic model for the Western God. The old man with the flowing beard is a comforting image, but not acceptable to most thinking, educated Westerners. A non-theistic model of God does exist within Christianity. Paul Tillich, a 20th Century theologian and philosopher, introduced understanding God as the "Ground of Being." I like it. It is difficult to understand Tillich, but others have done an excellent job of making his concept workable in more common language. I would suggest reading the work of Bishop John Shelby Spong for a more contemporary understanding of Christianity in such a world as ours. I have also learned much from Buddhism, which doesn't have a God concept, but has a wonderful articulation of the nature of reality, our "attachment" to that reality and the power of compassion.

The bottom-line is that we have to choose our understanding of the universe, and therefore our concept of God. Today, we have all the major and minor religions of the world available to us, and as we are in need of explanations and answers to our questions, we get to choose. We no longer are born into a single choice, which we must become or reject. We truly can choose.

We can choose to accept the unknown, embrace the mystery and allow ourselves to *Be* within and a reflection of that mystery. We can give the mystery a name for both ease of conversation and comfort. I use "God." I choose to live a God-centered life. But it doesn't matter to the order of life. Any designations are ours to make, for our purposes.

Understand that I am not making light of religion, but I am recognizing the reality of the historical pattern. We create a system of belief to explain that which we cannot explain to our satisfaction and comfort. I believe this to be a good thing. We clearly need organization in order to survive and live together. Without some structure, most people would simply not do well, and chaos on both the individual and cultural levels would reign. We need to be able to organize our world, which includes our understanding of the universe, in order for us to make sense of who we are and how we are to be.

In recognizing the pattern of religious choice within our cultural and species evolution, I choose to own my responsibilities in making choices. It isn't an external God proving me with answers; it becomes an internal God demanding that I own my life and my choices. It also allows me to understand that other people will make different choices that work for them, and that is okay. I prefer that they not impose theirs upon me, and I'm confident they hold similar sentiments. But we all get to choose.

What is our place then, in the cosmic dance?

I haven't a clue. Remember, it's unknown. I have opinions, which I hold as beliefs, and I organize my world about them, and they allow me to survive and work well with my fellow travelers on planet Earth. And I *know* that they are opinions. Good ones, well founded, and well developed at points, and still, opinions, not facts.

There is a lot of freedom in that knowing. It allows for constant maturation and evolution of thought, whether brought about by reflection, insight, readings, dialogues or bolts of lightening. It allows for a broader acceptance of variance, and it allows for growth through the constant search for understanding. I don't have to defend it to someone else's death, nor do I need to convert others to my way of viewing the universe. It is my choice as to how the cosmos works, and I get to live with it and by it and people know me through it.

Humans are delightful creatures. We appear to be unique in so many ways, so many of which are marvelous and others of which are quite dreadful. We are born, we evolve as individual creatures in a remarkably short period of time, and we die. In addition to all the activities that that process generates directly, we attempt to explain and understand it all, applying meaning and insight to all stages of pre-birth, birth, growing up, aging and dying. Perhaps other species do the same, but we are either not aware of it or have been unable to effectively communicate with them. Therefore, we have decided that only the human species is capable of such action. I suspect a case of arrogance on our part, and only time will tell.

Are we alone in the universe? Seriously doubtful as far as I'm concerned, but if it makes you feel more secure, believe it. On the other hand, until we make contact, I would suggest not to worry about it. Focus on the task at hand, namely, living your life to the fullest. You are unique, and at least for the life you are living, you get to make all the decisions.

I believe that each of us has a soul. I have no idea as to its start or its end, but I believe the maturation of the soul to be a constant journey of growth and enlightenment, perhaps concluding with a complete merger with the cosmos or God.

In my cosmos, living life is a lot like going to school. I believe that we are about maturation and evolution, and we get to practice this life after life. As a consequence, we make choices about what we wish to learn and/or develop and/or experience for our maturation, and choose conditions that will allow those lessons to happen. The bummer is that we rarely remember the set-up upon entering the dance of life, and we have to explore and choose our way throughout our entire episode of life. Sometimes we do really well, and other times we have to repeat a lesson. But, it is of our choosing that we do so.

The outstanding thing about being human is that it is the place where the soul truly exercises the freedom of choice. I suspect that in other dimensions and/or worlds, the soul learns other lessons in other forms. But within the human domain, the actual doing is always reflected in choice, the ability to evolve positively or negatively. Whether we take a giant leap forward, a slip sideways or a falling behind: that is the risk, the challenge, and the joy of being human in this cosmos.

We don't *know*, and yet we must *choose*. As we own our choices, all of our choices, it often appears that each choice simply generates more questions to be answered. Don't be discouraged or over-whelmed, and as I've advised many a student, simply do one paper at a time until you've completed all of your work. In subsequent chapters, perhaps you may find additional clues that aid you in your journey of a life filled with choices and options.

mega/mini choices/anchors

Among my many opinions, I hold a couple that I consider to be principles. Principles hold a special place for me, for I find them to be more universal in nature, which is to say I believe they apply to all humans, not just to myself.

One such principle is that of choice.

One of the unique aspects to the human school for the maturation of the soul is the opportunity for free will. Each of us has the constant opportunity to make choices, and we do.

Some choices we make prior to entering this life cycle, establishing the basic parameters that might best serve our lesson plan for this episode. However, those choices generate only the basic framework. Such choices could include the country and culture, the time in history, the genetic code of the parents, the local community and the sub-culture of tribe and/or family. This is the stage upon which we are choosing to act out our lives. Again, I believe that we have certain lessons that we wish to explore, and I do believe that there is not a fixed script. If everything is a given, then why play? Where's the growth? Where's the opportunity to make decisions?

It appears that we forget what we know from other dimensions when we enter the physical life cycle. Actually, I suspect that there is a progression of forgetting that takes place as we assimilate to the life we have chosen. Perhaps babies actually still remember in vivid detail the conditions that they just left, and are complete sponges in their need to become part of this game of life. Some of the most interesting questions I've heard have been from children between the ages of two and four, with the rare one occurring as late as six. I'm sure the Zen Master stole the famous "What did your face look like before you were born?" from a local three-year old. At some point, we usually forget other realities and believe that this life is the only one.

And this life is about making choices. Sure, it appears that many are made for us as we grow up, and yet we always have the option of revisiting each choice and making new ones. That's what seems to keep therapists in business, not to mention, most religions! That raises an interesting question: has therapy become a religion, and are therapists today's shamans? But I digress.

Just to complete the overview, upon death we have the opportunity for more choices. I suspect that judgment does take place, but it is the committee of "me, myself and I," who evaluates the work. And rather than the classical sense of judging, it's more like a review of lessons learned, comparing with the original game plan, and considering options for further work on some of the same or new material. Then it's choices about the where and the when and which world or dimension that might best serve the soul. All the time, making choices! I believe we have guides and teachers who assist us in this process, but I'll discuss that a bit later.

The primary focus of this chapter is to look at the choices we make as conscious, functioning beings, as "adults." That is not to diminish the importance of the many choices made for us and by us during childhood, for most maladaptive behaviors emerge from childhood experiences and the choices we made in response to those experiences. However, we have the opportunity and responsibility to examine and modify our ongoing responses, i.e., choices, to any earlier experiences of our lives. Ultimately, we own our choices in the "here and now," and if that requires reframing parts of the past, that is still a present time action. This may require the assistance of a guide, friend or therapist, but the choices are always ours. For many of us, it is part of the act of reflection, a tool that I will discuss later.

We make thousands of choices daily. The good news is that the vast majority of them are made at the unconscious level. Studies indicate that there is a relatively narrow amount of "mental space" that is available for conscious choosing, approximately 12%. That means that 88% of the activity of our "consciousness" takes place without us thinking about it. Again, that's very good, or our ability to function in this modern world would be greatly diminished. For example, ever drive home from work and wonder how you got there? A common experience - and one that reflects the fact nothing unusual happened requiring conscious thought or action. The "automatic pilot" is one of the best features of being human.

It is also the source of many of our problems. The best analogy for the unconscious I prefer relates to computers. The unconscious is like a huge, extremely fast database. When a stimulus makes contact with us, either external or internal, the database does a sort to find a previous experience that best matches the stimulus, and sets the machinery in motion for our response, which is typically described as a reaction. This process is completed in micro-seconds, using primarily the primordial portions of the brain. It has allowed us to survive. From a species perspective, if we had to consciously choose the appropriate response to the charging saber tooth tiger, we probably would be deleted from the gene pool. The bottom line, again using the computer database model, is the rule of GIGO: garbage in, garbage out. If we fill our unconscious with options that do not work well, then we will be constantly plagued with "bad luck" and errors, errors of bad choices.

The conscious portion reflects the work of the cortex, which analyzes data, looks at options, and makes conscious deci- sions. It is the job of the conscious to decide if the reactionary choice made by the unconscious is the one that works best, or if it is time to develop additional options. I seriously embar- rassed myself years ago by simply walking down a hallway in which I thought I was alone and was relatively lost in reflection, when a young friend jumped out at me. I nearly punched him before I got my reaction under control and opted for a more appropriate response. So we both were embar- rassed, laughed and moved on (though he never attempted to surprise me in such a fashion again, so obviously some lessons were learned!).

This conscious work includes reviewing the patterns and habits generated during childhood, especially emotional, communi- cation and interpersonal habits. When someone says, "that's just the way I am" it really means, "that's the product of my life's habits, which I choose not to change." Basically, we "choose" almost all aspects of our being. Our emotional state is a choice. How we interact with others is a choice. A favorite maxim of mine, which I stole from my friend Paul is, "the effectiveness of your communication is measured by the response you receive." Clearly this applies to communication, but you can substitute the word "communication" for any number of nouns and verbs, such as "leadership," "compassion," or "spiritual practices."

We have the power of choice. We make choices about every facet of our lives. We are the product of our choices. Our choices can never be taken from us. They dictate our identity and our state of being.

Personally, I've a few choices I'd made in the past I'd like removed, and hopefully all those who have been potentially hurt by those choices either have forgiven me, or are, at least, ignorant of their existence. The flip side of having the freedom of choice is taking responsibility for all choices, both conscious and unconscious. Most of us like the notion of freedom of choice, but are more ambivalent about having to be accountable for all the choices we make. Yet that appears to be the rules for playing in the human life cycle game. We get to make choices. We get to live with the results, both good and bad. Whether opportunities for growth and maturation, or opportunities for slip and slide, we get to own them all. No wonder the soul likes this game! It isn't fixed, the outcome isn't known, and it always goes down to the wire. What fun!

At times, we make choices I call "mega-choices." These are the choices that set the course for what we want to be. They can be positive or negative, but they are the guiding benchmarks against which we measure all others. On a daily basis, we make mini-choices that either further align us with our mega-choices or take us off course. A simple example is dieting. To choose to modify one's eating patterns for the desired result of less body mass is dieting. Choosing to diet is a mega-choice, one that will influence much of our daily routine. The daily routine then becomes a series of mini-choices about our alignment with our mega-choice of dieting. We call this "staying on the diet" or "falling off the diet." Regardless of what language we use to describe our choice-based behavior, we still own the consequences for our choices, both mega and mini.

Choosing to follow a particular religion is also a mega-choice, sometimes referred to as a "conversion experience." Such choices may determine values, beliefs and behaviors and thus, life altering, hence mega. But having made the mega-choice, the game is not over! For every mega-choice, we get to make thousands of mini-choices that further define the mega-choice and effectively reprogram the giant database of our unconscious. Imagine the warrior who becomes a Buddhist, and accepts a life of non-violence. The number of conditioned habits that have defined success as a warrior that would require re-examination to be the non-violent Buddhist would be fascinating and complex. Not only would physical reactions require modification, the individual's very thought and analysis process would require re-work, not to mention the emotions (or lack thereof).

When I was young, drugs were as popular as they are today, and many community Christian churches attempted to "save" young people from their drug habits by converting them to their sect of Christianity. I generally supported the action, for it seemed the lesser of evils. And yet if the conversion moved the responsibility for the individual's life from drug-dependence to Jesus-dependence, then the ultimate outcome may be similar for the soul. I suspect that no major lessons are truly learned if the responsibility for one's mega-choices is not owned by the individual. I believe that each of us owns the maturation of our soul, though any given life cycle may only deal with a limited number of issues or lessons.

We all make mega-choices. I vote for making them as consciously as possible. This would include mega-choices we "inherited" during childhood, in which we get to consciously review and modify them as necessary. Sometimes this requires assistance and support, and it is still our choice to do so.

I also suggest that these mega and mini-choices define who we are for this life cycle only. It is difficult to apply our human ethics, values and judgments to the needs of the soul. Remember that I believe we lose awareness of the pre-birth game plan, so we must always make the most ethical choice. However, we need to guard against becoming too proud of our "good behavior," for it may only apply to life on this plane of existence. The rules for good human interaction may not always align with the lesson plan for the soul's maturation and growth.

This analysis may actually have some Biblical backing, though rarely considered. I took a graduate class in the historical teachings of Jesus, an academic attempt to determine what words within the Bible might have actually been spoken by the historic person. We examined the phrase, "And the first shall be last, and last shall be first." This phrase shows up in several different contexts, with the authors' attempting to interpret the phrase. The phrase itself, however, may be original. As I reflected upon this phrase, it struck me that another interpretation could support multiple life cycles, or some form of reincarnation. It seemed a logical statement reflecting the laws of karma. When I shared this thought with the professor, the answer I received was, "if this was a World Religions class, that could be true." What a wonderfully politically correct comeback for a seminary professor! The bottom line is one of perspective, what appears to be the best possible choice, mega or mini, in the human sphere, may not meet the needs of the soul. And still, one must choose.

One of the phenomena that I observe about myself and others is the ability to allow mega-choices to simply slide off our radar screen on a regular basis. It appears that our small window of consciousness also includes a limited time frame. We make the choice, we act upon the choice, we build new patterns and at times, the whole thing seems to float out to sea!

Apparently, making the choice isn't sufficient to fully incorporate the direction and/or focus into our lives. For the transition to become complete, we must add the skills and practices of life discipline.

One of these skills is the generation of "anchors." Anchors are specific actions and/or thoughts that evoke a state of being. We all have many anchors, both positive and negative. Have you ever heard a song from high school, and you suddenly return to a former moment? Strong memories have strong anchors. There's one song whose title escapes me, that whenever I hear it, I'm once more driving home from my job, late, on a warm summer night in Los Angeles. And I smile.

And then there are odors or sounds that lock in a particular memory, and you're once more in that moment. For many people with less than positive relationships with their parents, the mere sound of "that voice" is enough to set them off. And so anchors are formed, and they affect our daily lives.

We also can consciously choose to create an anchor. At one time in my life, my commute included passing by a spot where I could clearly see the local foothills. I used that visual reminder to ask myself the question, "How do I wish people to experience me today?" The good news is that I usually answered the question with some positives! Today, I still use a version of that anchor as I'm preparing for work. If I fail to do so, the odds of my being slightly "off" increase, for I've not clearly established my proper intent. The anchor prepares me relative to my intent and focus for the day or event. Literally, the anchor is the conscious programming of the unconscious database to align with the chosen directives.

We can create anchors for ourselves, and we can also create them for others. A simple touch may anchor a state of being, and the repetition of that touch returns the person to that anchored state of being. I have witnessed individuals who were clearly unhappy as I entered their space, and in a matter of moments, using an established anchor, their entire mood would lighten and becomes more positive.

Anchors can be varied. Some examples include: a touch or gesture, a specific sound or tonality, a dance step, or a phrase, a laugh or whine, or a posture. They can be triggered by locations, times of the day, or people. They are yours to create and use. Perhaps a starting point would be to simply become aware of your current anchors. They exist in your unconscious, ready to act at a moment's stimulus.

I suggest that you create anchors that support your mega-choices. If your mega-choice is to have its fullest impact upon your life, then you will need to have a way to quickly remind yourself of that choice on a regular basis. My belief is that annual renewals are not sufficient. These are nice, yet not sufficient to keep oneself in alignment with the mega-choice. Too easily they become the annual New Year's resolutions that disappear in mid-January. Daily anchors, conducted as quick rituals, are best for ensuring alignment with the mega-choices of one's life.

many paths to the summit

There is no single path to God.

No one has the definitive path, the one way all must follow to find God.

I know those statements will seriously offend a great number of my friends and family; others will consider me the evil one for even harboring such thoughts; still others will be sad that I am so easily deluded; while others will be relieved and happy.

So be it. But that is "truth" as I understand it.

I've already said that I believe we have a soul. The soul is eternal. The personalities going through this particular life cycle are not. The soul is on an eternal journey of growth and maturation, perhaps ultimately becoming one with God. In the course of this journey, the soul uses many life cycles within the human dimension, and perhaps other options in other dimensions as well. The soul, in conjunction with its guides and teachers, reviews the progress made within each experience and decides what is the next best choice for its development.

I have no proof of this, for it is just like every other human belief system. It is part of my belief system, and it forms the basis for the decisions I make every day.

There are many interesting theories as to how this process actually works, even within my own worldview. Some believe that the soul has many "lives" happening simultaneously. These lives occur during different times in history concurrently, connecting through the soul and feeding the soul's growth. This would explain "past lives" in a totally different perspective! Each past life would actually be lives occurring in parallel with yours, just in a different time/space continuum. A very fascinating theory, and one that would set modern psychology on its side. It attempts to explain changes in an individual's state of being that are being generated by another being in another time/space dimension as connected through their common soul. It would be like, multi-dimensional counseling!

Traditional Eastern views, based in Hinduism, would argue for an unbreakable progression of the soul through various states of maturation, as well as social position. The rate of progression would be controlled by the choices made each round, as governed by the rules of karma. This can take a while. When asked how long, one spiritual leader said, "As long as it takes a sparrow, flying over the mountains once a year, carrying a silk scarf, to wear them down into a plain." I suspect that is a very long time.

Bottom line, no one knows the path to full maturation of the soul. I would suggest that this is a liberating condition, not one that generates fear or despair. In fact, those who will defend their way as the only right way, even to the point of justifying others' deaths in the name their God, I suspect are being driven by fear, certainly not love.

We certainly face a number of significant challenges in the course of our life cycle. One that we all hold in common is death. The consciousness of our own mortality may be the source of philosophic and religious thought. It isn't apparent that other species are aware of their death as an event that is coming. Death is certainly a reality, and other species clearly work hard at avoiding it and mourning the loss of a dead one. But they don't appear to be concerned about it in some sense of self-awareness; they simply live in each moment. Perhaps this is a lesson for us to learn, as opposed to assuming they are the clueless ones. However, we are aware of our mortality, and this awareness drives us nuts!

What happens after we die? Is that it, or is there more? Was there a purpose in all this life beyond the living? These questions generate a massive fear of the unknown. That great "unknown" factor just eats away at us. We want to know. Not knowing, we make up stuff. Really good stuff, but nonetheless stuff. Then we organize our lives around the stuff, including our personal lives, communities and entire cultures. Then, just to make sure that everyone believes it, we smack those that don't "believe" really hard. If that doesn't work, we may go as far as to kill them. Then, only our view remains and we can be at peace with our choices about the order of things. It's only because we are afraid that we behave so poorly. Fear is a powerful, unconscious driver. People often think that if another view of the universe is allowed to exist, then perhaps mine is not correct, and then what? Life has no meaning, or it has been wasted, or our belief system will somehow collapse. Look at the Inquisition and the Crusades as examples in history. Assuming that you don't believe they were strictly motivated by land grabs and politics, consider the cruel torture, pain and death heaped upon individuals, families, communities and cultures. What was the basis? My religious views are correct and yours are wrong? There is only one correct form of expressing a devotion to God? What is fascinating to me is that relative to the Crusades, both Christianity and Islam profess love and compassion as their foundation, so what an interesting expression of love. Another factor to consider is the relationship between ignorance and religious fervor. Certainly during the time of the Inquisition and the Crusades, the literacy rates were extremely low, and the understanding of the "holy scriptures" was left up to the interpretation of the religious leaders. This appears to be true today in most "fundamentalist" movements including Christian, Muslim and Marxist alike.

Given the knowledge we have in the 21st century, how is it possible to hold such a simplistic understanding? We have the remarkable opportunity to view many histories and cultures and religions over the last say, five thousand years. How many exist today? How many have disappeared? For those that have survived, to what degree have they continuously evolved? And throughout, has the world collapsed? Has humanity disappeared?

No. Life goes on – constantly creating new conditions for life possibilities and expressions of understanding and reality.

So, no one *knows*, and this is liberating. Liberating because it reinforces the freedom that we have to make choices. Scary because we have to own our choices, and be responsible for them, if ultimately only to ourselves.

If we choose to believe in the reality of a spiritual life, then one of the primary tasks we own during the life cycle is deciding how to go about it. I would argue this is a mega-choice based upon another mega-choice of believing that humans have a spiritual dimension. This is part of being human, part of the experience of the life cycle, and a key to how, and how well, we will dance this time.

"Many paths to the summit," is an expression that I believe originated within Hinduism. That would make sense, given the vast plurality that Hinduism encompasses. There are many positive lessons to be learned from even a brief study of Hinduism. I still consider Huston Smith's *The Religions of the World* to be an excellent overview of the major religions of today, and would recommend it to anyone interested in such an overview of the options available for consideration.

Hinduism suggests that there are four major paths or options for achieving spiritual attainment. Each path has literally thousands of sub-options that have evolved over the centuries, including other major world religions. In general terms, the four major categories include: 1) jnani yoga, the way of the mind, 2) bhakti yoga, the way of the heart, 3) karma yoga, the way of work or doing, and 4) raja yoga, the way of direct experience and experimentation. Recognizing that there are significantly different paths for an individual to consider and choose allows for each person to find the discipline in which they are most attuned and comfortable. In short, the goal is to make the wisest and best possible choice for the most effective growth and attainment. Metaphorically speaking, there are, in fact, all kinds of holes in which the variously shaped pegs may fit.

Let us take a quick peek at each of the major paths. Each is a yoga, or discipline, with a particular approach to the spiritual summit. Each allows for a different orientation and approach to life. For many in the West, the word yoga conjures up images of people doing strange movements with their body. This is called hatha yoga, and is used in many other disciplines as a basis for bringing health and control to the body so that the spirit may evolve. Yoga is the generic term for discipline, and is often connected with spiritual disciplines. What I like is that the disciplines reflect my observations of human nature and the various patterns of how we learn, process knowledge, and develop our unique skills and abilities. Some people approach life through their intellect and development of mental capacity; others are more comfortable in dealing with emotions and dedication of the heart; others prefer to focus on doing things and the actions of life; while others need to get in there and mess with the process directly, generating their own experiences and knowledge. No one path is better than another, all lead to the summit. Choose the one that works for you. Today, we have the freedom to use the discipline that best matches with our personal characteristics for growth and learning. What a magical time, there is more than one way!

Jnani yoga is the way of the mind, or the power of the intellect. This discipline attracts folks who are serious thinkers, needing to know the structures and connections and the basis for all that they believe. Logic and clear rationale become standards by which they examine the various stimuli, and there is an equally clear direction to support the choices that are rendered. As a spiritual discipline, it requires a keen understanding of the principles that one uses to live by, and then the practice of constantly applying these principles to every thought, word and deed. Probably the practices of meditation and contemplation are very useful, focusing on key concepts and phrases that allow for a continual maturation of the subtlety of one's basic life principles and beliefs. It is not sufficient to be brilliant and knowledgeable; one must also apply that constantly evolving knowledge to each moment of life, and each decision. It is reported to be a "short, but steep path" to the summit, with many potential pitfalls, particularly if one is unbalanced or unhealthy in any aspect of life.

Bhakti yoga is the way of the heart, or the power of devotion. This discipline attracts folks who lead with their feelings, acting from the internal sense of connection that is centered in the heart. Though I speak of an emotional basis, do not confuse this with our Western psychological understanding of emotions per say, but rather an orientation of sincere and constant devotion. The focus of these aspirants is generally through a particular bodhisatva, a spiritually advanced being, who has returned for the purpose of assisting others in their spiritual journeys. Every action and every thought is an expression of devotion to their God, their spiritual leader. Christianity is viewed as an excellent example of bhakti yoga, and would be considered an appropriate choice (among many) for those most comfortable with this path of spiritual discipline. This may explain why Christian missionaries have never truly converted Hindu based cultures. Hinduism simply embraces Christianity as an acceptable practice within its larger context. Some speak of this path as approaching your God as a lover, with full dedication and openness of heart, committing your mind, body and soul to the endeavor. In the West, we are very uncomfortable with our sexuality, and attempt to divorce sex from the spirit, so such thoughts are more problematic. But in the East, sexuality is at times considered an appropriate option to utilize in becoming closer to God.

Karma yoga is the way of work, or the power of our actions. This discipline attracts folks who need to be doing, taking action, working on some project or task. Certainly they would ascribe to the old saying, "actions speak louder than words." The path for them is built upon each and every action that is taken. Every action aligns with their beliefs, or expresses their devotion to their God or spiritual leader, and never to pull attention to themselves. The focus on doing is very grounded, and focuses on achieving goals and accomplishing tasks. In modern business terms, the discussion is often centered about the product versus the process. However, karma yoga is not a system of outcomes regardless of process, for each action is crucial in and of itself. Therefore, one may be working toward a clear goal, but how one gets there is equally important, for each step is part of one's spiritual path.

Raja yoga is the way of direct experience, in which you yourself become the malleable instrument of God. It is also known as the "royal path" because it requires complete dedication of one's life to the process, for you are the experiment. Hatha yoga is foundational to raja yoga, and aspirants are capable of amazing control over their bodies as the result of the advanced, focused training and practice. There are stories of masters literally having themselves buried for weeks, and emerging alive. Others have sat without clothing on a glacier for days, without freezing. These masters do not do these acts for purposes of personal glory, but to demonstrate their supremacy of will over the limitations of the flesh. In raja yoga, the body becomes the experimental and experiential basis for union with God or the cosmos. This work requires lifetime dedication, and aspirants embark on their journey with an established master and only focus on the work. I don't believe you can follow this path and have any other occupation or family responsibilities, nor would you care to do so. This work is your life.

Though I like the analysis that Hinduism offers, one does not have to become a student of the East to attain spiritual enlightenment. The key is to understand that there is simply more than one way to God. If the worldview you were raised in doesn't work for you, it simply may be an inappropriate methodology for your preferences. Find one that works for you.

It is a mega-choice to believe that we as humans have a spiritual dimension. I have made that choice, and I base my life around that understanding. It is a choice that is fundamental for many in the world. How it is expressed is as varied as the world's population. What is liberating is to fully recognize that each of us is on our unique journey, and have the right and responsibility to make the best possible choices for our journey. That includes the path that works for each of us as we work our way to the summit. And it's okay if our journey matches with others, and we're able to travel together, whether for a short time or a life time. It's equally okay if our journey is different from our neighbor's. We are a communal species, though we need not march to the same drummer. We each own our individual choices.

truth about angels

Angels have recently become quite popular again. People have them hanging from the corners of their rooms, their rear-view mirrors and their jacket lapels. They clearly come in a wide range of styles, colors, shapes and meaning. The perfect accessory to life!

But do angels exist? Are they real?

Sure. No. Who knows? It is simply a bit difficult to tell the "truth" from this side of life. Perhaps upon the transition of death we'll have a better answer.

My opinion is that they exist, but not in the popular sense of a winged cherub, or a winged, mighty warrior. I recognize that in both certain Jewish and Roman Catholic traditions, angels are thought to be significant forces in our universe. They are carefully illustrated, with full job descriptions by rank and clas-sification. This has been the basis for some of my most favorite movies, and if they are correct, boy, am I in trouble! And this world is a lot more scary than I've experienced it to be!

Generally, my sense is that angels, traditionally defined, were part of our understanding of the universe at an earlier time, when our Western understanding of God was that of a human, white male deity, called God, who sat upon a heavenly throne. This throne, though magnificent, was amazingly modeled after thrones that mirrored those used by the current civil and spiritual leaders. And in a similar manner, God's court was organized in much the same manner that those courts of human history were organized. Either we projected our experiences onto the heavenly realm, or God was also into organizational development and just didn't take credit for it!

It follows then, that in God's court, there were angels. And like most courts, these subordinates had roles and rank. Now I don't pretend to know all of them, but trust me, there was a bunch. If you're interested, do the research, or minimally watch some movies such as *The Seventh Sign*, or *The Prophecy*, or *Constantine*. Actually, the details are quite fascinating. But the main point is, these angels were not necessarily nice. They were angels! And they were part of God's court, the inner circle, the confidents, the folk who for eternity got to hang with God. And apparently, hanging with God was not sufficient, so very humanistic alliances and plots and wars developed and lasted forever (remember, we're talking eternity factors here). In fact, the devil himself is a "fallen angel," and God's former favorite according to some texts.

And jealous! The primary source of jealousy was rank, generally referred to as "favorite." That is, God's favorite. This was sufficient for most of the angelic plots and twists until humans entered the picture. Apparently court worked just fine, and then God got creative and produced Adam, then Eve, and suddenly had a new favorite! Talk about the apple of his eye, humanity (referred to as mankind, women didn't count yet) became the end all of God's focus.

What happened? Some stories say God stopped talking to the angels, others say he gave humans a "soul" (something angels don't apparently have or need, but now want) and certainly he gave them his attention. Logically, this produced a new focal point for the jealousy of angels, and many a good movie plot!

Obviously, I don't buy into this worldview. I get it, and I understand it's place in history, and I enjoy lots of the metaphors and story lines, but I don't see it as a basis for today's reality. It certainly was a basis at one point in time. Remember, at one point in time (lasting for a really long time), the world was tri-level, especially in the West. Heaven was above, Hell was below the surface of the earth, and humans were on the earth. Trapped between heaven and hell, humans were born of the earth, starting with original sin (earth connection), and obviously closer to hell than to heaven. If one did really well at critical junctions of life, then one might be able to enter the Kingdom of God, also known as heaven. And remember, this was a definition of the reality of the universe. Not a metaphor or a symbol, the real facts of life.

So how did we make ourselves stand out from the angels? How did we convince ourselves that our short, tiny lives have meaning in the vastness of eternity? How did we compete with wings?

We built a new story, we became God's favorite. I can almost visualize a tiny human being sticking his tongue out at the angels, and doing that five-year old dance, complete with the "na-na, na-na, na-na" song! We became God's favorite, with honors given only to us. And we were honored in God's court, and had a home in his mansion.

Humans = 1, Angels = 0. And who's competitive?

So, angels were pretty magnificent creatures. They continued to evolve along with our understanding. Somewhere, sometime, somehow, perhaps in the age of industrialism and emergence of science, they became cute. They became our hidden helpers. They became small.

Makes sense, given how we humans took that Biblical "dominion" thing just a little too far. All creatures big and small, land masses, resources, water, air - why not angels?

So are they real? Do angels really help us?

In my understanding of how life is organized, we do have "angels." I have absolutely no idea what they look like, or even if they have any substance that one could look upon. For me, they are neither winged creatures of mythical proportions or cute cherubs, rather they are entities that have chosen to assist us. So, it makes more sense to me to call them "guides" or "mentors" or "teachers."

I have no clue as to why such entities would spend their energy working with us, and yet I consider it a distinct possibility that they do help us. The "why" would be best explained within your own belief system about the universe.

Since I believe that human life is like attending school, the school of choosing and practicing, and we have developed lesson plans that will aid in the maturation of the soul, then "guides" make sense to me. Schools are not attended, or run, in a singular fashion. It takes multiple entities. Some of us are students. Some are teachers. I suspect we work in teams.

I further suspect that these teams will interact in different roles through different life times, helping each other's souls to evolve and mature.

I also recognize that this is my opinion and may well not be true, yet it is the basis upon which I organize my life. It may be accurate, and it may have huge holes in it, but it works for me. It is also based upon my limited experiences in this world — direct experiences, not second hand.

I know many individuals who are acutely aware of and converse with their guides. Sometimes these individuals become practicing spiritual coaches and psychics, and their ability to assist others is impressive. I'm not one who can directly converse, but I do believe that others do.

I have had sufficient direct experiences to understand that I'm not alone, and that the team model makes sense. Be careful when you say to someone, "You're not my mother!" Perhaps not this round, it's just that old habits die hard! As I become more comfortable in my understanding of life, the connections with others become increasingly clear. And my intermittent interaction with psychics generally confirms the linkages. I used to spend a significant amount of time researching the texts, meeting various mediums and attempting to determine the "truth." Now, I tend to accept, and do, and be.

As part of my complex understanding of life, I may choose in another round to be a guide in a non-physical aspect to another entity playing within the school of life. I don't know if I have the credentials to do so, and yet my understanding of the school allows for the possibility. It is clear to me that I have guides, mentors, teachers that are not of this plane. It is also clear to me that they have taken on a major effort!

intent/thought/word/ deed/reflection

I am a process freak. If something catches my curiosity, then I want to know "how." This is particularly true for most things that deal with how we operate as human beings.

I remember an expression in an action hero novel I read in high school that used the phrase "stone cold glance." I thought, "Cool, how do you do that?" This started a small quest that led me to a book on eye movement and its meaning, and the mechanics of it. In turn, this led to practicing eye movements that produced both the "hard stare" and the "twinkling eye." Both generated by conscious choice rather than the physical result of an inner emotional state. Weird?

Not really.

We are a complex being, incredibly complex. Looking just at the body - what a magnificent, interconnected mass of systems! And our understanding of how this amazing system works continues to evolve. Modern medicine continues its exploration of the details, taking us into the emerging world of genetics that will allow us to impact the total system through the tiniest part. At each step of advancing knowledge, we often have to give up an old belief of how something operated, and replace it with a new fact, that will in turn, undoubtedly, be replaced by a new fact sometime in the future. Did you know that at one point, bathing was considered unhealthy? Good for the perfume industry, good for germs, bad for health. Taking sick people, putting them in closed environments, not washing them and bleeding them, was believed to lead to health. In that reality, only the strong survived. And that wasn't warfare; it was ordinary life! Fortunately, we've allowed new "facts" to alter our understanding of "reality."

Part of our human complexity is understanding the "whole," and how the whole is impacted by its parts and vice versa. In my early simple views, I started wondering about the mind/body connection. Note I neglected to include emotions as part of the starting point, demonstrating my ignorance! One of my early memories is that of reading the essay, "As a Man Thinketh." And if memory is correct, the primary point is that how one thinks shows up in how one acts. This was potent stuff for a 13 year-old kid. This got seriously embedded in my conscious and unconscious processes. Within a few more years, the idea of the connection between "thought, word and deed" became equally planted, adding not just more dots, but the nature of the interrelationships, and the issue of ethics.

I realize that over the next few decades I developed my understanding of many more facets, including: an understanding of the power of emotions; the impact of environment, both personal and cultural; the connection to spirit; past lives; constant evolution; the nature of things; and yet, I really hadn't moved beyond "thought, word and deed." My preference in counseling is generally based on behavior, with an emphasis on what you do as both a starting point and a benchmark for progress. I've a strong dislike for the word "why," especially relative to human interaction, for it generally leads to rationalization and excuses. I want movement, growth, positive change, not wallowing. Yes, we all have pasts, so learn your life lesson. Make new choices. Develop new habits. Become new people today, now!

In my constant quest for the "how" of life, I did not stray far from the complexities of "thought, word and deed." And I still don't.

Deed is the practical measure of our lives. The key word is "what." What did I do? What didn't I do? What did I say? What didn't I say? What was my non-verbal message? What was my energy? What was the impact of my presence?

When push comes to shove, I always start with what took place. It avoids the trap of lying to oneself, a very easy trap. One of my ethical principles: never lie to yourself, though it may be okay to lie to others at times. I don't hold that truth must always come first; I hold that compassion may over-ride truth, but that's another conversation in the balancing game. Back to never lie to yourself. If you're going to truly evolve, it must be based in the foundation of self-truth. Any deviation leads down the path of delusion. Now, please don't confuse this with beating yourself up or exposing your truth to the world or even another human being. Those are different issues, and are not necessarily useful. Keep in simple: don't lie to yourself, ever.

We do, of course. We all lie to ourselves. We lie about how we look, what we said or meant, how we really performed, what our motivation was or how we feel. The easiest way to lie is to accept the words of others, whether they are words of praise or criticism. I lead lots of workshops, and I certainly enjoy hearing from participants on what they got out of the workshop. It makes me feel good, gives me an energy push and increases the glow. But I gave up evaluations, for I know better than anyone else in the room if the material worked and what I brought to the session. I accept that I may not have presented at the top of my game, and folks still got a lot out of it. Cool. But no lies, it may have been a 10 in their books and I'm glad, but I know it was an "8 day" for me. Lessons to be learned, improvements to be made. Let me be clear: I'm not into being hyper-critical, that's a potential dysfunctional trap. I simply argue for not lying at any level. That also means accepting doing really well. You get to have a 10, too!

Back to deeds. What a powerful starting point, one that can be verified by others. It also allows you to work a variety of levels. Examine the sample questions again. What did I do? What didn't I do? What did I say? What didn't I say? What was my non-verbal message? What was my energy? What was the impact of my presence?

These sample questions alone allow you to explore your own stories at levels ranging from the practical to the subtle, from the observable dynamic of communication and interaction to the sensitive areas of psychic connectivity. By starting with deeds, we will know that we are dealing with some element of our lives that is real. Not a figment of our imagination, not a possibility, either negative or positive, but a real component of who we are as an individual being.

Deeds also become the benchmarks of our development, whether positive or negative. They lend a bit of objectivity to the process. We can measure them in real as well as subtle ways. Want to know if the diet is working? Weigh yourself, remembering that scales do, in fact, lie and are out to get you! Others can also provide you with feedback. "You seem more happy these days." Yes, your smiling more and looking at others with positive intent *is* paying off.

The human being is a complex and integrated entity. What happens in one dimension shows up in others. The body impacts emotions that impact the mind that impacts the emotions that impact the body that impacts the mind in an endless loop of connectivity. It is often more difficult to chart the course of the mind and emotions, so by carefully observing the products of the body, we may discover the benchmarks of deeds. And deeds become the gateway to the more subtle arenas.

Mentioning the mind takes me back to the thought component of "thought, word and deed." As I mentioned earlier, I recognize I have a bias towards the "head" as a starting point. An equally powerful starting point is the "heart," and even then the head gets involved in translating the purpose and message. Thought takes us into the wonderful world of the psyche, and how we organize our view of ourselves, others and the world.

Thought is the complexity of our inner world. Thought captures the interplay of emotions, beliefs, values, self-image, imagination and choice. We all know the power of the phrase, "Perception is reality." Where does perception take place? It lives in the land of our inner world, weaving its own story out of the complexity of our unconscious and conscious, mixing hard facts with the filters of our personal mythology. We own the reality of our inner world just as much as we own the reality of our behavior, thought and deed.

One of the important lessons I learned while taking some training in Gestahlt Therapy was to separate the realities of the inner and outer worlds, what is going on in the privacy of our minds and the dynamics of normal human interaction. One of my fellow trainees was tormented by his self-judgment of his fantasies, which did not match his perfectly acceptable behavior. I don't remember the specifics, but they dealt with some sexual interactions. None of them were real in terms of past history or current realities. They only existed in his head, and he decided they "just weren't right." His judgment, based upon his value system and religious beliefs, deemed himself not only unworthy of love, but also questionable as to his leadership role and even being borderline evil. This self-image generated from a quiet, gentle, helpful, caring individual as experienced by others. The instructor/guide and the group worked hard at assisting him in understanding the fantasies are just fantasies, and that he should recognize them for being just that, not real behaviors. Acceptance of that inner reality can then lead to its transformation, if that is what is desired. Of course, a few of us in the group argued for keeping the fantasies, they were great!

The trick is when we translate the world of thought into the world of interaction. For most of us, this is positive. We believe that caring and love are good foundations, and we develop strategies for implementing those values into behaviors. We believe that helping others is positive, and so teamwork becomes a new way of conducting business. We believe we are connected to other living creatures and our world, and environmental issues become critical both for ourselves and those who follow.

For those whose translation is negative, they end up in therapy or the criminal justice system. Both options are designed to assist individuals in translating their inner world into a more acceptable outer world reality. Unfortunately, those in therapy and the criminal justice system have about the same success ratio. But it is good that the effort is made. Success is always dependent upon the choices of the individual and their ability to identify options, generate good implementation plans, and integrate their world of thought with their world of deed.

There are literally thousands of books, workshops and retreats all designed to assist us in our pursuit of a healthier, happier inner world. I certainly have my opinions as to what works and what doesn't. Bottom-line, I am pleased that so many options exist, and that we recognize it as an area in which we need to play. I'm not going to attempt to cover my thoughts on all that exists in the inner world, and what to do about it. This may require another book. At this time, it is central to be aware of and sensitive to the role of the inner world, the world of thought and its impact upon who we are, and how we are experienced.

So what is the role of "word" in "thought, word and deed?" I probably don't pay as much attention to this portion, but my thinking tends to go in two directions. *Word is the articulation of experience and the translation of the inner world to outer realities.* I addressed the translation of inner to outer realities a bit above. To summarize: the behaviors, the words we say, the acts we do, the deeds of our lives, are all a reflection of our thoughts, of our inner world.

One model of how we operate suggests that there is pyramid of values, beliefs and emotions that move us toward knowledge and abilities that result in an external "doing" evidenced in behaviors, statements and presence. One of my favorite expressions is one I have modified from Richard Bach's *Illusions*: "argue for your limitations and they are achievable." When I point out to someone that obstacle they are facing in achieving their specific goal resides not in others, but in their own head as a belief, they are shocked. That old mantra of

"I'm not worthy," runs true for nearly every person at some level. We all process, or translate, those beliefs and values that are at the core of our individual and collective identities into the realities of our personal and cultural lives. Perhaps this is most succinctly captured in the world of rap with the exclamation, "Word!"

Word is also the articulation of human experience. For better or worse, simply experiencing life is not sufficient for us humans. We must discuss it. Hence, "let's talk." Is there a clearer path for ending any meaningful dialogue than that expression when introduced between two individuals, particularly anyone in a "meaningful relationship?" But I digress.

The Zen student in the pursuit of zatori, the state of enlightenment, practices in multiple ways. Upon achieving some level of experience, the student must share this experience with the master in determining if zatori has been achieved. Generally, the answer is "keep working." Perhaps when zatori is achieved, the need to ask is also removed. But the point here is the need for articulation.

There is a compulsion, and some argue a requirement, to translate experience into a higher level. That is, to put into words that which we have experienced in our physical, emotional, mental and spiritual worlds. Without words, the act of sharing is limited given our current evolutionary state of being. We like talking. We like writing things down. If we aren't able to do so, we're not sure it really happened, and it becomes really difficult to share with anyone else. Now, should we develop telepathy as an alternative means of communication, perhaps words, both spoken and written, will be transformed. But for now, words are the primary means of sharing, especially key concepts, beliefs and values that form the basis of our identities and cultures.

There is a paradox, however, and most truth has an element of paradox. Words are by definition, limited by their cultural index. So how do you explain that which is outside the framework of the words with the words themselves? Will we borrow words from other cultures, such as two I've used in this chapter, zatori and gestahlt? If so, then we start doing disclaimers, noting that we're pointing in a direction, not quite this word and not quite that one, but somewhere in-between. And, in case you're not confused enough, we can go on spiritual retreats and be instructed to get beyond the limits of our conceptualization (inner words) in order to directly experience the ultimate Is. Tricky, eh?

Regardless, as humans we are still generally stuck with the need to articulate and translate our experiences and the dynamics of our inner world into the external realities of expression. So, we talk. We write. We email. We IM. We continue to search for a relevant means of articulating the conceptual into the concrete. Word.

Thought, word and deed are critical to the development and growth of a human being, and hopefully, the more subtle maturation of the soul. But in my more recent considerations, I realized I needed to expand my model to include two more steps, the bookends of thought, word and deed. These are the steps of "intent" and "reflection."

Intent is the focal point of will. It is the conscious set-up of the great unconscious machinery of the functioning human being. It is the foundation and command central. Even if we're unclear on the components, our intent can still get the whole working in the direction and manner we desire.

In "mega/mini choices," I used the analogy of how we work like a computer. Our unconscious functions as a huge database, responding to every stimulus with a response that most closely matches a previous response in our life. This reactive response is sometimes good and sometimes bad. It is always reflective of our experience and represents the best the database has to offer. Our conscious awareness functions as the programmer, making choices among options, setting up software and focusing on specific elements of the overall operation. If we had to make every choice of our lives consciously, we would quickly be over-whelmed and the entire operation would shut down, becoming dysfunctional and unable to effectively interact with our environment. This human mechanism is truly marvelous relative to its integrated systems.

In accordance with adult learning theory, in order to integrate new ideas, we go through four stages: unconscious incompetence (I didn't know what I was actually doing was wrong); conscious incompetence (so that's what is causing the problem); conscious competence (I can do it when I am thinking about it); to unconscious competence (it is now on automatic pilot). It requires the 12% conscious to run the process so that the 88% unconscious can "learn" the new, desired responses. Another way of stating this is in order to form new habits of how we respond to the world we must consciously practice those new habits until they become "natural."

Now, I can teach you (as can others) how to break down all the little steps, and assist you in developing options for new behaviors, etc., yet often we don't have the time, interest, commitment or energy. The alternative is to use the master program, our intent. Clear intention is the setting of the master program both to outcome and style, as well as state of being. Once clearly set, the machinery will generally operate quite well.

The trick is doing the intention thing well. Again, it is critical that we are truthful with ourselves. Our intent is not what we think should be the proper response, but the one we truly want to come into existence.

In my management consulting practice, I often get asked to coach managers on how to effectively deal with non-performing employees (generally performing quite well, just not in the desired direction). My first question is always, "What is your intent relative to this employee? Do you want to save him/her, or get rid of him/her?" Now, in our politically correct world, we always want to save people, just not in the real world. For the manager who really wants to get rid of the employee and says they want to save him/her, they are breaking the principle of lying to oneself. The result is that the employee will read the real intent quite clearly, and immediately not trust any response emerging from the manager's mouth. "Word!" So, be clear on your intent.

Okay, for those of you wondering how one truthfully deals with the non-performing employee whom you want to get rid of and still maintain positive style, here's the starting articulation point: "Your performance is not satisfactory. [Add some reasons or standards as needed, and keep it to the high points.] If you do not change your behavior in a significant and immediate manner, I will pursue your termination." Sounds harsh, but nearly all people will get the truth and intention, and respond accordingly. That response may be greatly varied, including a positive change, initiating their own immediate job search, or engaging in open warfare. Be prepared for all the alternatives. And remember, even when delivering harsh messages, you still own your choices about how you conduct yourself relative to presence, tone, manner and caring.

Be clear on your intent. How do you want people to experience you? What is the purpose of your meeting? Presentation? Family talk? How will you conduct yourself? In what manner?

After you answer questions like these, then visualize yourself doing, being, feeling, talking and interacting. Practice in your mind, the imagination is a wonderful tool. Say it out loud; for the act of articulation is often less clear than initially visualized. And by the way, the unconscious database cannot differentiate between real experiences and ones generated in your imagination, so build positive responses!

As you practice this practice, it will take less focus, time and energy to establish intent, and you will create anchors to assist you. Then a simple exercise or ritual may re-enforce or return you (if you've strayed) to your desired state. For me, I use a simple breathing exercise, conducted in the space of one breath, to remind myself of being appropriately centered as life gets busy and harried. As I approach any job, I ask myself how do I wish to be experienced, and what is the focus of this particular encounter. Consciously choosing sets the intent, then the automatic program kicks in and you generally get the desired outcome in the desired manner.

Now, the other bookend is reflection. *Reflection is the evaluation and consideration of thoughts, words and deeds.* It is also the opportunity to reframe that with which we are not pleased.

We all do reflection. There is no event in our lives that at some later time, sometimes seconds, sometimes years, that we don't go "Hmmm." Sometimes it is simply a random thought and other times we enter into an evolved and delineated process. But it still happens.

Not surprisingly, the principle of not lying to oneself again comes into play. As we reflect on any event in our lives, it is important to conduct an honest analysis. If something doesn't go the way we desire, we must break it down, figure out what didn't work, and create new alternatives. Then practice those alternatives in the imagination so that they have as much weight in the unconscious database as the actual experience. If it went exactly the way we desired, still assess what worked and re-enforce the positive. I strongly urge you to not practice the American habit of harsh judgment on yourself. Unfortunately, our culture is very quick to judge, both ourselves and others. We can debate the source of this bad habit, and I'll suggest religion, and yet the reality is we still leap to judgment. Let judgment go. Rather, accept what is. Consider it carefully, and take appropriate actions, even corrective actions when needed. Beating yourself up simply doesn't help, and only leads to dysfunction. Functioning folk assess, take action, and move on.

I should point out that the above comments are heavily process in nature, and do not reflect issues of values and ethics. I am assuming positive intent throughout, but in all honesty, the process will still work should one have negative intent. Negative intent, the desire to hurt others, cause pain and suffering, is generally not considered the best benchmarks for spiritual maturity. I would always urge you to consider positive benchmarks of love, compassion, caring, appreciation of all beings and a sense of unity. However, the process works regardless of the flavor of the intent. This may be very useful to remember if you're assisting someone who is in a negative pattern.

At another level, reflection is a discipline. It requires setting aside time for the purpose of examining the status of one's life. It allows us to examine our mega-choices and the alignment of all the mini-choices. It provides an opportunity to assess if we need more tools for dealing with specific issues, and how those tools might be integrated into our lives. It provides moments of consciousness about the flow of our lives, and whether we are still heading upon the course we have chosen. It is maintaining the "big picture" in the midst of all the band-aids that our lives' melodrama generates.

Some friends of ours have just returned from their annual, month long retreat. How marvelous that they can pull this off! I'm totally jealous. They return renewed, full of energy and purpose. They have spent conscious time in practicing healthful physical activities like yoga and meditation. They have studied sacred texts and reflected upon the implications for their lives. They have chosen to enhance and prioritize their spiritual practices.

Yet I wonder at my wonderment. Haven't spiritual masters always conducted themselves as such, and called us to do likewise? Jesus was reported to meditate and pray regularly. Buddha was reported to spend three hours of every day and three months of every year in meditation and reflection. The models exist in every tradition. Yet we struggle with it in our hectic lives, filled with meetings, work, school, soccer practice, birthday parties, exercising and PTA meetings. It's time to reflect on reflection.

So now I have described the five-step dance - Intent, Thought, Word, Deed and Reflection. There is a flow. Each impacts the other. Each is related. To be balanced requires some attention to all. Then, the sum is truly greater than its parts.

karma: instant and otherwise

Karma is one of those words that we borrowed from another culture and language and immediately started changing its meaning. I suspect the most common usage of the word in America is in conjunction with another word, creating the expression "instant karma." I actually like the concept of instant karma. It seems to work for me, whether in understanding one of the dynamics of life, or in the use of song lyrics.

"Instant karma's going to get you," is, I believe, the song lyric, and having it written by John Lennon certainly aided in its usage. As interpreted by John and those following, "instant karma" aligns well with a couple of other one-liners that have stood the test of time – "You reap what you sow," and "What goes around comes around."

Per my observations and direct life experiences, these phrases appear to work a fair percentage of the time. Unfortunately, the timing is often not obvious, and so we frequently don't get to witness some misbehaving person getting their just due, but it does seem to happen ultimately. Those who live violent lives and beat on others, often end up getting done in by someone more violent. (Isn't it interesting that we also tend to think of these phrases as applied to individuals who are being nasty?)

Since I'm curious about the truth of sayings that survive, I wondered about the mechanics of instant karma. Here's how I think it works. As a human being, we put out energy constantly, sometimes it's a general feel and sometimes it's very focused. It is experienced by others as raw emotion, or actions, or combinations thereof. People respond, and most match the energy coming at them. If someone walks in the door and starts yelling and cussing at you, you generally respond in kind and an argument ensues. It may even lead to a fight. A shop owner who keeps a gun behind the counter will generally attempt to use it when confronted by someone with a gun. Results vary.

Still, in a very simplistic manner, it becomes clear that what you put out is generally returned in kind. I think most of us get this, especially when applied to dramatic stories. And when the story is an action story that leads to violence, we can all sit back and say, "instant karma" or "what goes around comes around." At other times, we tend to forget this simple truism. There was a current news story that is unfortunately all too common. It is about a family that is very upset with the local police because their son was killed in a fight at 6:00 a.m. on New Year's morning. The police know who killed their son, but arrests haven't been made. The family clearly thinks it has racial overtones. In their legitimate grief, the family is ignoring that the evidence indicates that their son and some buddies spent New Year's Eve roaming about the streets hassling and mildly beating up other groups of people. Sounds like fun for guys on a party night. They simply ran into another group that didn't cooperate. Instant karma.

But back to the truism of what you put out is generally returned in kind. I suggest the real power in this dynamic is not in the dramatic, but in the mundane. Return to my constant question, "How do you want people to experience you?" Beyond working towards a consistent alignment of intent, thought, word and deed, there is a practical element as well. The energy you put out, the manner in which you conduct yourself, will be reflected in the faces of those you are dealing with. By choosing to be positive and sharing some expression of love, support, enabling power, comfort, friendliness, calmness or any other positive behavior that works for you, you will receive a similar energy flowing back to you. "As you sow, so shall you reap," which is a farming reference for those of you who have never had the opportunity to grow things.

Think about this. Doesn't it make ultimate, practical sense to foster a friendly environment with the people you hang? It just makes the day-to-day a whole lot better. Now, please understand that I'm not suggesting that we do that phony, sugary thing that everyone in the room sees instantly and starts to gag. We always need to respond to the dynamics of our environment in an appropriate manner. If someone is visibly upset, isn't it more appropriate to put out a caring, concerned response filled with neutral to warm sound and perhaps even a supporting touch, than to crack a bad joke and giggle? And yet I've witnessed folks do just that. I assume they are too uncomfortable with their own energy to respond more appropriately. And yet walking into a room with a smile and a genuine interest in the people present is returned in-kind most of the time.

Perhaps instant karma needs to be changed to constant karma. As part our mini-choices that support our mega-choice as to who we wish to be, we need to develop an awareness of our instant feedback loop of constant karma. If we're wondering if we're being who we want to be, it doesn't have to be a cosmic mystery. Simply, honestly observe the responses of those you encounter every minute of every day. There is your benchmark. There is your mirror.

I teach a variety of communication skills that center around the development of the observer that I discuss in more detail in a future chapter. Part of the deal is the need to practice, and though one can practice anywhere anytime, I like to work with real places like the grocery store. Now, I'm not suggesting overt, dramatic encounters, unless you just like that sort of melodrama, just regularly acknowledging or saying "hi" to folks in line and aisles. Putting out a friendly response that reflects something very real in that moment will generally get one back. Like standing in the aisle, staring at the never-ending selection of cookies, and wanting to pick one. Noticing that a fellow shopper is in a similar state, I simply observe, "They just give us too many choices." And a pleasant exchange and smile takes place that even includes a wistful comment from the individual that it "applies to more than cookies." Now, isn't that better than just reaching over his/her shoulder and grabbing the Oreos?

Instant karma to constant karma, I like that.

But that isn't the original usage of the word. In fact, it is a long way from the original intent, as I understand it. Karma is a major principle found in the religion of Hinduism. It is the cosmic application of the principle of cause and effect. It is set in the context of a rigid system of reincarnation that was further supported by an even more rigid societal caste system.

It works like this. As an entity, one progresses through a process of constant evolution. It starts with the animal kingdom and moves into the human realm. Apparently humans are better than animals. The progression of the entity is fixed through the animal dance, and becomes variable once it moves into the human. The progression is still fixed, for one doesn't get to leap over social classifications from life to life as reflected by the caste system. But it becomes variable because one faces the possibility of one step forward, two steps back. One can screw up in this lifetime, and should this happen; one must pay in the next. This is the law of karma. People then enter life with a karmic debt that must be repaid in order to get back on the proper progression. Ultimately, the holy man has made it through the entire chain of progression, is free of any karmic debt, and is living a sufficiently pure life in which more debt is not incurred, and he becomes free from the cycle of life.

Personally, though I've heard karma and karmic debt discussed in a variety of traditions, including the current new age movement, I generally don't agree with many of the interpretations. In my worldview, we do get to do multiple lifetimes, so I believe in reincarnation. I don't believe the progression or cycle of lifetimes is fixed. Remember, I look on life as participating in Earth School. As an entity that is about soul maturation, we "learn" our lessons in a variety of formats. One of them is Earth School, and it is the place of choice that leads to character enhancement and development of the will. To effectively work on these elements, one needs an environment filled with options and choices. The life work is figuring out what are the correct choices for the soul's maturation. Again, the earlier Biblical reference I used, "The first shall be last and the last shall be first," would apply to my understanding of reincarnation. The choices that appear to be obvious choices with positive human outcomes could be made with the wrong intent, so it works well in the human arena, and doesn't win points in the soul arena.

In my understanding of the dance, we get to make choices throughout. That starts prior to our birth, in which we select the "stage" that is most appropriate for this session's lessons. We do this in a team environment. Some members are guides and coaches; some are necessary players. We may choose to enter a life for the select purpose of assisting a fellow teammate in their lesson plan, and they may return the favor. Remember, with multiple lifetimes, the pressure of cramming it all into one is significantly lessened. And aren't we all willing to help out our buddies? According to a recent psychic reading that my wife had done, I was her father in a previous round, and the old habit of giving advice, I still haven't given up! But I'm learning.

Each round we design with our team has some objectives. These are the lessons we will attempt to learn in this school session. We may do really well, and move on to other soul work, or we may need to try again. We are the "judges" of this life, with the assistance of our coaches. So I see a distinct connection between teammates in any given life, and like actors who appear in multiple movies together, the different roles demand different relationships. That may appear as karmic debt, and it may be the cast simply switching to a different role for the current movie.

Now, I am totally willing to believe that karma works exactly the way it was originally designed for those who use that particular worldview as their basis for soul maturation. I simply find no evidence to suggest that there is only one correct worldview. It would be like having only one movie playing with one type of script. I like comedies, other folk like heavy dramas, and others live for the true horror film. That's okay with me. Diversity is good, monotony is bad, and life is diverse – if anything.

In my worldview, we get to design the game, set up the players and choose the playing field. Then we "forget" all that and enter the game and attempt to make the right choices so that our soul continues its maturation. There is a purpose to every life cycle – it is the soul's journey. It is much easier to play when we keep perspective, and understand the rules. Like constant karma.

love, energy and light

Love is the most important word in one's spiritual journey, and it is the word that we have made a major mess of in our American culture. Go figure!

For a moment, consider the most common usages of the word today. "I love those shoes." "I love that show." "I love that actor." "I love you." Actually, most of the time, the word love is closely tied to the word hate. "I love these shoes, hate those." "I love that show, hate that one." Love has become a measure, the balancing point to hate. How many children in a fit of anger say, "I hate you" to their parents.

My, how fickle we are, and how loose we are with our language.

Personally, there was a period in my life in which I refused to use the word. It lasted for more than a decade. In part, it was my personal protest against the cultural "blanding," or dilution, of the word. In part, it reflected my inability to commit to another. In part, it reflected my respect for a word that I knew demanded more than I was capable of articulating.

I got over the commitment problem, finally! But boy, did it take a lot of practice. I am fully and sincerely capable of saying to my wife, "I love you." Though on an irregular basis, I still have to translate that common phrase into my true understanding of its meaning. Sometimes I do it only in my own head for my own clarity, and sometimes I say it out loud, so both of us may be clear. However, adding a whole bunch of words to attempt to accurately capture the personal experience of love isn't always politically correct! It's also much easier to say, "I love you."

Love is a power word. It deserves respect, care in its usage, no dilution.

As for the blanding issue, it still bugs me, yet I've learned to endure and limit my rants to moments of mild intoxication. But I avoid participating in its usage. I find other, more appropriate words. "These shoes are extremely comfortable and way cool. Those suck." Yes, that works better for me, and seems to convey the desired message of love and hate. For hate is a power word also.

We struggle with the word "love," even within our traditional religions. In the West, focusing primarily on Christianity, love has been debated for centuries. Three major categories emerged victorious, all in fancy sounding Greek, which translates love into three categories: sexual, communal (more literally, brotherly), and theistic, or God focused. I get that, and can relate to all the categories. It certainly becomes easier and more comfortable to ascribe categories of love to our relationships. If you participate in any Christian religious sect, whether Roman Catholic, Eastern Orthodox or Protestant, loving God is the very basis of the religion. *"You shall love the Lord your God above all others."* It is interesting to note the reference to other Gods, which says something for the competition in the authors' times, but we can apply it to other aspects of contemporary life as well. Its application might cause a serious amount of heartburn for most Americans, in light of the high value given to money and the toys money makes available. Regardless, the theistic love of God still stands in the Biblical texts as the primary and foundational category of love.

Then, for Christians, the next category of communal love may face challenges with that "loving your neighbor" problem. What if you have a lousy neighbor? What if that neighbor tends to drink a lot on the weekends, obviously turns deaf as a result, and plays his music at very high decibels late into the night. Perhaps it's a religious experience, so you let it ride. But loving him? That's a challenge, a real challenge. Thank God the interpreters stepped in and explained this category of love in a more general way, allowing love to be for the mass of my neighbors, not specially the goofball next door. Yes, this allows love to become more manageable.

And sex, the final category of love, the almighty eros. Well, most of us find the personal expression of love to be pretty cool, and work hard at maintaining a reasonable level of participation. Sometimes we're challenged about doing it with the same person, and some folks have issues around gender, but we generally manage to keep love in sight. I do get concerned about the peering into thy neighbors' windows to ensure that no rules are being broken. I mean, come on, it's challenging enough in our hectic worlds to actually practice love at the personal level without worrying about the rules. Unfortunately, given our American cultural attitudes concerning sex that frankly baffle most Europeans, love at the personal level is too often too difficult a subject to even discuss.

So, for me, the categories are a part of the blanding. They allow us to not be responsible to ultimate power of love, to set arbitrary boundaries and limits that more closely reflect our tribal laws rather than an understanding of the nature of love. The categories are useful in working through the complexities of relationships, not in understanding the nature of love.

So what is this word, love? It is four letters that attempt to capture the most powerful force in life. And as is always the challenge with the articulation of the direct experience, the word falls short. To get to the experience, we have to add a bunch of other words, and it just gets too messy. Back to my wife, when I say, "The profound joy I experience in being able to share intimately with you the life sustaining energy of love is absolutely amazing and I am overcome with wonder," is simply too long. Although, at the right moment, it might win me points!

A central key to getting it straight with love is understanding at both the head and heart levels that we don't own it. Love is not a commodity. No one gets to have control over it. No one can hold it in their hand, or give it away or take it back. I can give you my heart, albeit a bit messy, but I cannot give you my love, for "I" have no love to give. There is no "my." Now we've reduced the problem to two letters, one little word. To truly allow love its rightful place, we have to give up, forever, its possession. We don't get to say, "my."

Sit with that for a moment.

Try visualizing yourself not using the word *my* in conjunction with the word love. The phrase "my love" goes away. Love doesn't go away. Love never goes away. It is a constant. Our ability to - be a part, be aware, be sensitive to, join in, be a vessel, pass it on - changes, and yet love stays.

Love isn't personal, our experience of love is. And it is such a tasty, heady experience that we want to hold on to it, to own it, and keep it forever. Unfortunately, that's not the nature of love, and like fireflies in a jar, the experience of love can pass, as if the light goes out. We must remember, love is larger than we are. It was here before each of us, and will still be here when we finish this round.

If love isn't personal, then what is it? Think about your own experiences of love for a moment. The look of your significant other, the sunset that touches your soul, the realization of being a part of thousands of people standing shoulder to shoulder, the joyous greeting from your dog that signals another dog eternity has passed. Love is in all of life. Love is the glue of all of life. Love is *energy*, boundless, endless energy. It is the nourishment of the soul.

So I use energy as a basis for my understanding of love. We tend to understand energy. We get it. Though try and hold an electron in your hand, tricky, eh? As physicists go farther out, or in, to quantum physics, what are we learning? At some point, the scientist and the mystic meet, and they are in the same space studying the same dynamics of life. It is energy and it is love. And like the Energizer Bunny, it just keeps on going and going and going. Kind of like the relationship between kids and water!

We live with the fact that we move energy around. We may not know how it works, but the facts of modern life are based upon energy moving around. Electricity, as one form of energy, is generated somewhere, and it gets sent down lines, moves through transformers, and gets divided into working pieces that run our toys. We cannot see it or hold it, but man can we feel its kick if we make the wrong connection! And look what happens when the power goes out - birth rates go up! Love is energy in transformation!

I'm very comfortable talking about individual people's energy fields, and I think that conversation is becoming more common. Individuals put out different levels of energy. Having said that, we tend to experience that variance in a couple of ways – on one level, it appears to be a constant that some people put out more than others, almost as a part of their genetic make-up. At another level, it varies within each individual in the natural course of events, mood swings, physical exertion and focus. I would suggest that it is also a matter of choice, supported by practice and technique. There may well be a genetic variance among individuals, and yet each individual has a lot of say over how it works within oneself. I'm not going to teach the mechanics of energy manipulation within this dialog, but techniques do exist. Some are mechanical, such as the control of breathing. Others blend the dimensions, such as found in meditation. Others use the vastness of the psyche to spin new webs and make connections. The bottom line is that one can modify the impact of energy as it flows through oneself.

The phrase of "going with the flow" has more power than we suspect, and at times we do get caught up in the flow of energy around us and are seemingly carried away. But flow is an accurate starting point. Energy flows, as does love. We can participate in that flow. It can be a small trickle or a thunderous waterfall. We have the power to choose, not to control, but to participate. We can transform the energy of love, increasing its impact and focus, as long as we maintain the flow.

Did you know that light is both a particle and a wave according to physics? That's downright paradoxical, which means there is a truth lurking about. Isn't it interesting that both energy and love are often described using variations of light. A blinding light, a brilliant flash, a shining ball of energy, a glow that warms the very heart, are all descriptions of love and of energy. To understand love, we have to accept its paradoxical nature. It is very real and the basis of life, and yet you cannot hold it, touch it, measure it or own it.

Light is the basis of the halo ascribed to holy ones, a shining glow that surrounds the body and is able to transform or heal other bodies with simply a touch, a transfer of energy. There is a Tibetan healing discipline through which its practitioners effectively diagnose and heal patients using only the aura, the human energy/light field that emits from each of us. Now that's pretty cool! For them, it is the result of vigorous training and discipline; for Saint Francis, it was the result of prayer and connection with God.

Love is.

Perhaps we best understand it as we understand energy. Practice allowing love to flow through you, and see where the journey takes you. It is the key to the spiritual path.

learning vs. integration

I'm a bit of a head case, a Jnanist by preference. By that I mean that my preferred method of spiritual development is through intellectual focus. I prefer to take ideas, allow them to roll around inside for awhile, attempt to articulate them in different ways, and then figure out how to apply them in my daily existence. That's my preferred spiritual path. It's only one way, and as I discussed in "many paths to the summit," there are other equally valid ways of nurturing the spirit.

But given my leanings, I've had to pay close attention to this issue of learning. Having apparently missed out on the option of living with a hands-on master from whom to learn, books have been my primary source of information. Now, there have been many, many dialogs with teachers, friends, family, classmates and the wind, but the primary source for me has been the written word. The good news is that I like to read, always have. As a kid I consistently got in trouble for reading comic books under the covers at night with a flashlight, when I was supposed to be sleeping. Come to think of it, I still stay up too late reading.

So I read, anything and everything. I like knowing, so I read the newspaper, every day. I read magazines, handouts, brochures and books. All kinds of books: fiction, non-fiction, historical, theological as well as my favorite, science fiction. I even read a book on physics, though it hurt! Does this make me smart? No, just willing to read, and willing to explore new data.

And there is a lot of data out there. Just walk into your local bookstore and look around. What percentage of those books have you read? If you're like me, maybe 1-2% at best! So in my passion for learning, one of the first harsh lessons I realized was, I wasn't going to "learn" it all. It simply wasn't possible. Not for lack of trying, especially in the early years, but it's still a fact. So I narrowed the field, and applied my reading primarily to texts that fed my spiritual quest.

When I was in graduate school, I noticed, due to the school's ancient check-out system, that my good friend and I were the only ones reading the books from this one section. The section held books on the para-normal and the minority groups within the Christian tradition. We were particularly interested in the mystics, and before you think that too strange, I'll drop some big names into that group, like Saint Francis and Meister Eckhart. This was a source of great conversation for us, and many days we would cut class to wander in the botanical garden next door, and debate the possibilities of what we were reading. The common theme that emerged for us was the need to look at the whole, to understand the connectivity of all life, and that each individual must balance the journey of the self with the journey of the community. Pretty heady stuff, and just how graduate students should be filling their time! Oh, we also learned all of the regular curriculum too, but the joy was in our own searchings.

But I still didn't get all the books read. Oh, I tried, especially in the areas I found most interesting. There was a point when the New Age movement was just getting popular, that I could wander into a bookstore, and have read perhaps 60% of the material on the shelves. Today, I'm back to my 1%.

Now, I try to keep the brain cells working by reading at least one non-fiction per month, and as many fiction as possible, particularly science fiction. Science fiction, and within that genre, those books that deal with the human potential have always fascinated me. I so admire the writers who can take a bit of fact, and build a whole new possibility for our species. If it is true that we use only a small percentage of our brain, then what possibilities await us? I hold the hope that as a species skills such as telepathy and energy transfer will become commonplace. Then we'll have a whole new set of ethical and practical issues to debate.

So given my bias towards learning, I figured that if I read enough, pulled in a sufficient amount of data, it would some-how translate into enlightenment. I was and am committed to the spiritual journey, fully believing that as a human being, we have a spiritual dimension that must be fed and developed as much as our bodies, emotions and minds. So I "learned."

But there are problems with this path. You may already know them; I was just slow. One, you can't read all the books and sacred texts. There simply are too many, and besides, way too many languages to learn. Two, all that data can make you book smart, but so what? Yes, it makes you interesting at a cocktail party, but how does that translate into your actual spiritual journey? Three, it's a trap, or at least a potential trap, of hoping to find the answers "out there," with the perfect correlations, and if found, believing that that knowledge will set you free.

As these realizations grew, another response was needed, and the key was clearly present in all the literature. Beyond the product is the process. It is not sufficient to know of something, one must *know* it.

On the spiritual journey one must integrate the learning into one's life.

This applies to all skills, frankly. I teach a lot of communications stuff, and the more one integrates, the more "it" becomes a part of our unconscious response and who we are. And it is essential for the spiritual quest.

There is a tension that exists between learning and integration. Integration requires you to take a chunk of some truth, and apply it and practice it in as many ways as possible in your life. If compassion is important, then how do I demonstrate compassion in confronting an angry man who is willing to hurt someone? Or how would I assist someone determined to hurt him/herself? Is it better to allow someone to learn from a painful mistake, than attempt to prevent it? This is especially tough when applied to children we love. Does compassion mean passive or passionate? The questions of application are as endless as the choices life offers us. The trick is not to get depressed by the process, and embrace the process as the evolutionary journey of the spirit that continues forever, even into the next round of Earth School.

The tension that learning generates is found in the potential multiplicity of options. If you were to take a World Religions class with the hope of discovering the true meaning of God, or the commonality between all religions, you could easily complete the course with the following set of mixed insights:

- God exists not as a deity, but as the unknowable Is, and each person must become one with God.

- There is one God and the path is through his son, Jesus Christ, or the prophet Muhammed.

- This world is illusion, and the path is truly understanding the nature of this world, and in breaking the bonds of illusion, becoming one with the universe.

- There is a fixed progression of life cycles that is endless, and we must all move through the cycles in the manner proscribed by the natural laws that govern our journey.

Clearly, a good World Religions course would point out more options than I briefly noted, and the attempt to integrate those various "learnings" into your own integrated life may well generate some tension.

This tension is normal, and I would suggest it is a positive experience that will both expand your capacity for accepting the diversity of perspective among people while challenging you to become more articulate as to your own beliefs and understanding.

There are many ways to approach the maturation of the soul. Resist the temptation to immediately judge, despite your family and cultural conditioning. Resist the fear that is natural to being exposed to something unknown. Allow yourself to consider the possibilities, to enhance what you know or to provide greater clarity as to what works for you.

Integration is the essential process of figuring out all the mini-choices that support your mega-choices. It helps ensure that what comes out of your mouth matches your actions. It helps ensure that other people may experience you as a consistent, whole, healthy and happy human being.

I hope you welcome a certain amount of openness in your integration and that you will allow for continued evolution and dialog with new and different ideas. Avoid building walls of judgment and false superiority that allow you to hear only your own voice. The spiritual journey is a path with no clear end and many options. Each step offers a new opportunity for understanding and growth. There is a mystery to this journey, and that is a bit scary, for we all like to "know." However, I encourage you to embrace the mystery, and allow the rules of your process to be open and inviting. Consider, reflect, embrace, reject, integrate. All are parts of the maturation of the soul.

Play well!

teachers come in all forms

I've always wanted a teacher. You know, the great guide, the master, the one who would be able to direct my spiritual development, answer all my questions and generally move me along my chosen spiritual path. Kind of like having my own personal magic wand, even better, the rock against whom I could always lean.

Hasn't happened yet, but I'm hopeful. Some folks get lucky and have a lifetime with their spiritual master. There is a woman in New York that I've heard about, and a bunch of people are following her about, learning, growing, being. Very cool for them.

When you look at the ancient texts, it seems to me that teachers used to be the primary way. Folks would find the master wandering the hills or the halls, and just follow him or her, generally "hims" in most of history. Life was filled with dialog, examining the various issues, searching for truth, over-turning the old ways and creating new options. The master spoke, the followers listened and discussed, the word was spread via oral tradition first generally, and then written.

So, have we lost the teachers? Do we have them, yet choose to ignore them? Do we lock them up? Is our time not worthy of masters? Have they been replaced? Or have we evolved to a new way and time of being and learning?

It's a puzzle to me, and I've obviously more questions than answers. Still, I'd love to run into my master. The troubling question is, what if I already have?

So, based upon my limited exposure, I've a few responses to my own questions, just because I must. Again, what captures my attention is the nature of our current reality. One of the intriguing aspects is how small our world has become. Just think, only 150 years ago, the average individual did not travel more than 25 miles from their birthplace in their entire lifetime. 25 miles! Now, we go that far for good ice cream! Many of us drive that far daily just going to work and picking up the kids. My friends' 8-year old had a basketball game that was 70 miles away. It is almost impossible for any of us to imagine our lives being lived within a 25 mile radius. It just isn't rational or a conceivable reality for us.

Yet think of that former reality. You wouldn't know as many people, and the routines would become highly consistent. The seasons would be very predictable, and surprises would be limited. No wonder marriages were for life, you might be lucky to find even one person willing to put up with you! I mean, talk about a limited selection field. We can meet hundreds of people in a day.

And think about news. When the Civil War ended, some folks didn't know about it for months. Months! Today, world-wide events are on the evening news with direct video feeds. Earthquakes would happen, and folks would never know. Period. Just not know. Today, we are the era of global and instant knowledge. What a gift. And what a burden. One of the top fears of parents today is having their child stolen. Yet, according to FBI statistics, child stealing is way down compared to just 50 years ago. Why the fear? We know about it. If a child is kidnapped in Florida, folks in California will know about it that same night and be on the look-out. Kids are generally safer than a generation ago, and we are generally more fearful. Consequently we've changed our pattern child rearing. Parents are commonly present most of the time now, becoming playmates, referees and protectors. It will be interesting to observe the sociological impact on socialization skills over the next few generations, and how that will impact individualization, creativity and the societal relationship to authority. But I digress.

The fact is, the world is simply smaller today. Most of the time, I like it. Take religion for example, it used to be you grew up believing what your folks and community believed because there simply were not any other options. If my village was Hindu, odds were I would be Hindu, no questions asked. If I was raised Roman Catholic, I'd believe that was the only true faith. And the same was true for every religion in every corner of the world. The patterns grew, some religions took hold. Statistically, most of the West is Christian, most of the Middle East and Northern Africa is Muslim, Asia is Hindu, the Far East is heavily Buddhist, and Jews are scattered throughout along with the other significant religions. Growing up in those regions, individuals naturally thought there was only one way, and probably never even considered options relative to the "normal" religion, even if they had major questions.

It simply was the given norm. Today, we are exposed to all religions, and at least in America, we still have the freedom to choose, though that may be at increasing risk. So find the one that makes sense and works for you. It may resemble shopping, and hopefully folks won't just keep trading in their religion because it becomes uncomfortable. The point is that the world is small, our exposure and knowledge is wide, and we are able to make these mega-choices about how we organize our lives.

It may be in our new world reality of being "smaller," that we have lost our teachers. The single master no longer walks into our village, shares their wisdom, and has people follow in order to evolve. Today, the wisdom of hundreds of masters is at our Internet fingertips, or at least our libraries. In fact, we are faced with the challenge of information overload. How are we to make sense of so many viewpoints, each with profound insight and truth? It's not surprising that people become defensive, fearful of any challenges to their way of thinking and beliefs. It's simply too much information to assimilate. The need to create order out of apparently increasing chaos is substantial. People want to know and have their boundaries defined. I believe this is the basis for the revival of fundamentalist Christianity in the United States. Even in the face of contrary information, beliefs are clearly defined and stated. Lines are drawn in the sand, and comfort is found in locking arms together. This is especially clear as to the behavior of the fundamentalists of all religions. Keep it simple, allow for only one truth, and in the name of God commit any manner of social action, good or evil.

Obviously I don't think that way. I work hard at not being too tough on those who do. I prefer to remain open to the wonderful complexity of the universe and the expression of love and life and being.

Today, we have hundreds of teachers in many forms. It is a reflection of our small world. I've had the opportunity to read works of many great masters that have been written down and translated. I've read philosophers and poets from all ages, and my greatest thought provokers are often science fiction writers! We have information from the ages at our disposal. We have access to many masters, or at least the aspect of learning that is part of following a master - though we may still miss the presence and the actual guiding hand.

But perhaps that too is a condition of our reality that is reflected in the evolution of our spiritual development. Perhaps spiritual development is now to be owned by each individual, rather than being taught directly through a master. Perhaps we have evolved to a state of being, a state of consciousness and awareness, that we must own our own spiritual advancement. We are born in a time of amazing options and limitless opportunities. So it makes me ask, "What is the spiritual reality of this time?"

Given the lack of spiritual masters of the historic model wandering our land, how do we deal with the challenge? We choose. We choose to learn, to expose ourselves to whatever we feel called to undertake, and integrate that knowledge, the learning. Part of the learning goes beyond the sacred texts and stories, to the very processes by which that learning emerged. We need to understand not only the words and their meaning, but also the means by which those words were generated. Part of the learning is knowing our own processes of integration. I somewhat sheepishly have to admit I have an undergraduate degree in philosophy, for I am a lousy student of philosophy. What I did garner from that period of study was a better understanding of the process of thinking, of doing philosophy. That has become a useful life skill.

Since I suggest that our beliefs will either limit us or propel us, I live by the parameters of my belief in personal responsibility. I own my life, and all the choices I make. I've set up the curriculum for this session in the Earth School, and I will evaluate it upon its completion. I don't get to turn it over to anyone else. I am responsible. Now, as I discussed in "truth about angels," I'm not alone. I've got guides and teachers; they're just not physical. They're part of my team, before, during and after, and I'm a part of theirs. Even so, the bottom line is that I must be my own teacher, and own my own destiny.

We're given lots of clues along the way. Given the vastness of our world and thousands of people we meet annually, teachers simply are more subtle. As opposed to the single master one would follow for life, today we have teachers show up for one-liners or single events. It may be your taxi driver, your co-worker, your spouse, or your child. Lessons happen in grocery stores, malls, factories and places of worship. Simple moments of wisdom, dropped innocently into your lap at your time of need, offered by people, books, songs and acts of nature. I've had songs that pop into my head at just the right moment, providing illumination in the midst of angst. I have old favorite books that I'll read again, just to have that one line come up and smack me in the forehead. There are moments when the wind reaches out and sings to me the true meaning of constants, and I can only smile.

Yes, today, the real challenge is in recognizing the teachers. We've got thousands, and they're all ready to share their wisdom with each of us. We own the choosing, we own the being open to the possibilities, we own the receptivity to the messages, we own the integration, and we own the spiritual journey.

right choices/livelihood/ life style/balance

Can we have it all?

This basic question has plagued me my entire conscious life. I imagine that anyone today seriously attempting to lead a spiritual existence is equally plagued. I mean, I was raised in a relatively comfortable mid-American environment, provided all the basics of food, shelter and love, and offered a multitude of opportunities to explore. Like many of us middle-class types, I went through the period of student poverty, paid my dues and enjoy having sufficient resources to live a comfortable life style.

Yet my study of historical sacred texts seems to paint a picture of the spiritual necessity of rejecting the comforts of modern society, and embracing a life of poverty. Yikes, that just seems painful!

I didn't realize how deep and profound that irrational belief ran for me until I was doing some work on my own belief systems. As I've mentioned before, we all hold beliefs that will either propel or limit us. These tend to exist at the subconscious level, and generally require some event or some seriously focused work to bring them to the surface. For me, I was debating with a good friend yet another career change, and the aspect of earning potential was examined. My friend says, "So what is your comfort zone for how much money you can make? Fifty thousand? One-hundred thousand? Five hundred thousand?" I was startled, and wanted to say, "Unlimited!" But I realized he was correct, I did have a comfort zone. I realized that living in the part of California we do, $50,000 was too low, but I wasn't comfortable with $250,000. It somehow felt too high, as if it wasn't proper.

This required examination, which took months, and is still pulled off the shelf on a regular basis. Here's what I discovered. I had a belief that in order to be serious about one's spiritual journey, one needed to be in or near poverty. Somehow too much money was spiritually wrong, and would lead one astray. I don't remember consciously making the decision to hold this belief; it simply was there. And I acted upon it! Looking back at my careers, I noticed I would typically move on when I was becoming financially successful. Great way for my boss to get rid of me, just give me more money! Now, is that weird?

I chose to examine the source. And the source of that belief clearly was the product of my learning and cultural conditioning. I was raised Christian, and the early spiritual message hammerer into me was, "Jesus was poor, that was good; don't be greedy; too much money leads to evil." This was the product of years of simply listening to and reciting the Biblical stories with the church school interpretations. Buddha was my next big teacher, and he gave up class and wealth, and certainly taught that all this material stuff is the prime source of illusion, the path of non-enlightenment. And nearly every other writer, poet and teacher seemed to say, "Beware, wealth will lead you down the path of losing in to the spiritual game." So I absorbed the message, integrated it into my beliefs and created a powerful, limiting belief.

I've now decided that is not necessarily an accurate and/or needed belief. I've given up my vow of poverty, and chosen a vow of charity. It works more like this: "make it, be comfortable, give it away, avoid attachment." I like this one much better!

Money is a potential trap, *if* you allow it to be. I know, as do you, many people who solely focus on the attainment of money, having more of it and the toys it can buy. It is easy to become trapped in a cycle of perceived "need," a need that can only be satisfied by more. Needing bigger houses, more expensive cars, newer electronic toys, longer vacations, better retirement, private schools, gourmet foods and wines, the list is endless. The trap is so easy, that the obvious answer is to simply not go near it. That is the consistent message of the ancient masters. The path of least resistance is to simply avoid the conflict. And it certainly worked for them, so why not for us?

Actually, times are different, and different responses are appropriate. If you live in the United States, it is very difficult to take a complete vow of poverty, fully embrace the spiritual journey, and not be removed from society. In other times and societies, recognized religious aspirants were respected and supported. Food was provided and shelter was offered, often by folks who were only one step beyond the economic level of the religious aspirant. Think of any popular street corner where you live today, and imagine an individual sitting and placing a bowl for food in front of them with expectation that you will provide. Actually, we have that picture; we call them homeless. Most of us pass them by with a quick glance, sometimes a shudder; sometimes a harsh comment or thought, or sometimes we offer some spare change. We pass laws to keep them moving, and merchants generally hate them for discouraging customers. I don't believe any of us can contemplate a business model in which having homeless individuals posted outside the entrance would entice customers.

Similarly, to have a "vow-of-poverty" person approach any of us and ask for shelter for the night, generally would not result in an invitation to enter, perhaps a call to the police, but not an invitation to take shelter in our home, eat of our food and share our company. Yet some of us used to do just that if the stories of our early history are accurate. Different times, different stories.

A vow of poverty is challenging today. It would be very difficult to truly focus on one's spiritual potential and development from within a jail cell, mental institution or cardboard shelter with the pains of hunger gnawing at one's well being – at least for me! Perhaps it is time for an alternative, another perspective that allows one to truly pursue a spiritual journey without running afoul of the system.

I would suggest it requires a shift of belief, an understanding of accompanying sacred truths that can provide some guidance to contemporary implementation. What if the key is not in the reality of poverty, but in one's attitude and focus? What if the key becomes the force behind the lure of money?

I believe it is possible to follow a spiritual path in the midst of mid-America, but it is complex and requires constant vigilance and reflection upon one's intent, thoughts, words and deeds. It requires the development of a matrix of values and principles that work for you, and keeps you healthy and on your chosen spiritual path. Let's apply this to my "vow-of-poverty" issue.

As I mentioned earlier, perhaps it is not the money, but our attachment to money that is the problem. Sure, remove the money, nothing to be attached to, but even that doesn't necessarily remove the attachment. The key is attachment. The more subtle spiritual trap is attachment, for we all become attached to all sorts of things: money, status, position, physical condition and look, clothing, cars, computers, handhelds, sex, food, drink, drugs, houses, success, and, did I mention money? Attachment is a driver common to the human condition.

In our culture, some of the most common values often show up on license plate holders and stickers. "He who has the most toys when they die, wins." "Shop till you drop." "I'm spending your heritance." "Bigger is better."

Living in the Silicon Valley, one of the most common addictions or attachments I witness is work, and its accompanying need to be connected. People work all the time. Professionals will put in long hours, and then go home and fire up their electronics to continue working. Newer, faster toys appear every six months and must be purchased, because someone, somewhere needs to communicate with me, and only me, right now. That may be true for 1% of the population, and yet, for most of us, it is a trap. If you die tomorrow, you will be mourned and replaced. Life goes on. And will you say to yourself upon your evaluation of this round, "Boy, I'm sure glad I worked all those extra hours, Saturdays and Sundays, and vacations!" Yes, that may be the proper answer for you within this round of existence and for the lessons you need to learn, and if so, I fully support your journey. However, the giant "but" hanging out there is that I'm doubtful. What is often perceived as "duty" or "just doing my job" may be accurately an indication of attachment. The spiritual questions remain, attached to what? Is attachment desired?

The spiritual journey reminds to constantly review the basics, like making choices and owning them in all elements of our lives. I hear folks tell me they don't like their jobs or the demands therein, and find themselves trapped by the money being earned, the position or the total lack of obvious options. The Buddhist concept of Right Livelihood may need to be considered. The basic concept raises the question, "Is the career I currently am pursuing allowing me to be the person I chose to be?" The original Buddhist material actually provided a list of occupations that do not lend themselves to appropriate spiritual alignment, including careers such as arms dealer or camel dealer. Makes you wonder about our used cars salesman jokes. But back to the question of career, many people struggle with this one every day. Work is experienced as drudgery, painful and something to be endured. When this is the reported condition, perhaps it is time for an examination of the choices being made from a perspective of Right Livelihood.

What are the drivers? The true drivers, not just the first pass drivers of making money, providing for others or using a degree. Spend some time with the answers you offer up. Allow them to sit there for a while. See what else may emerge. Ask yourself, "What beliefs do these observations illustrate? What values are being reflected? How do they align with my sense of purpose? Are they real or are they possibly excuses of attachment?"

Only you get to evaluate yourself, so be honest. At times, brutally honest.

If you're a normal, functioning person in mid-America, you may discover that you have accepted a number of beliefs and values that have formed the foundation for your current situation. Upon acknowledgment of these beliefs and values, if they work for you, embrace them. If they are not taking you in the direction you choose for your life, then make appropriate changes.

However, take care in your changes. Particularly as applied to one's livelihood, the most immediate response is to find a new career or job. This is at time's the most appropriate response, and yet it is only one option. When considering the choices you own, remember you also own your emotional and psychological responses to your environment, and that includes your career. For example, Jennifer may strongly express her dislike for her job, and feels trapped by the income provided for her family. Her range of options may include: find a new job; stay with the current job and current feelings, though that may produce additional physical and/or emotional responses; change her emotional response to align with her stronger base value of family; or modify the conditions surrounding her job. We always have choice. At times, to serve the purposes of our spiritual journey, the choices may reflect the more subtle choices of attitude, values and response to the pull of attachment rather than the overt symptoms and indicators.

This is equally true for a consideration of balance, and I will discuss balance in greater detail later. However, it is a word that we frequently throw around today. "Work/life balance" is a common expression. It seems to suggest that work is not a part of life, and is perhaps a counter force to life that one must balance. I would suggest our lives are composed of a complex mix of components, activities, values, principles and beliefs. Balance reflects the resulting mix and ratio. There is no model of correct balance, right or wrong. I suggest it needs to be aligned with your sense of life purpose, beliefs, values, desired behaviors and realities of your situation. Working two jobs may be the best possible response to life at this moment, or taking a six-month break may be ideal. Only you get to decide, and then own the consequences of your choice.

Can we have it all? Perhaps. I am not suggesting that it is necessarily easy to follow a spiritual path and still be a functioning, successful person within our culture. The traps are many and generally quite subtle and difficult to ascertain and monitor. However, I believe that today the true journey is found in the examination and choices we make. It is not a blueprint that someone else gives us, and says, "Follow!" That is simply too easy, and we have matured as a people to a new understanding of what it means to be a whole person, responsible in all dimensions, owning all our individual and collective choices.

So, I gave up my vow of poverty, given to me, and have embraced my vow of charity, chosen by me. Thanks for buying the book.

balance: ebb/flow, consistency/centeredness, product/process

Sedona, Arizona is one of the most beautiful places in the United States. It is an interesting mix of an artist community, retirement community, new age psychics, ancient ruins, preserved hiking trails, amazing views, and really normal folk just trying to get by.

We love it, and find it to be a place of great renewal, a true retreat for the soul and body. It certainly meets my current definition of perfect hiking: get out on the trail sometime in the morning, enjoy a wonderful bit of exercise for the body, eye and soul, and get back in time for cocktails and the hot tub. Then make the big decision of the day, where to eat dinner!

We've been tempted to move there, or buy some small place to regularly hide out in, and yet what really seems right is to make an annual trek and spend a week. It adds a bit of balance to our lives.

Balance appears to be a goal of many of us, pursued with zeal, yet possessing many of the attributes of a greased pig. Just when you think you've got it, it slips away! It is an elusive state of being. Perhaps it is subject to the Fritz Pearl law of "you cannot be consciously aware of the emotional state you are in and be in that exact same state." That, by the way, is a very useful piece of practical information in dealing with emotionally distraught individuals. The very act of consciousness of an emotional state shifts it, maybe only a tiny bit, but it moves. Try it; it's true.

Maybe balance is subject to the same rule. If you become aware of feeling balanced, you're not. That is probably true if balance, for you, is an emotional state of being. For me, balance is not an emotional state for the most part. It certainly has a "feeling" to it, and may be a bit of an emotional state, and I certainly feel a sense of loss when I'm not being balanced. However, balance is more of a reflection of "state of being" rather than only the emotional state.

Balance is as unique as each person, for each person must define and find their own sense of balance. The very word implies forces that pull us in different directions. It becomes the neutralizing effect, the fulcrum point on the teeter-totter of life. Balance is an important word, and one that we all get to apply to our lives and the choices therein. Especially if we consider pursing a spiritual path, there are some interesting points of balance to consider.

Work/life balance is often a subject of debate today. As noted previously, it implies that work is not a part of life, but something that must be weighed against life. I suspect this is a debate that rages mostly in offices and professional settings, for many people who are working the trades and labor-based jobs understand the discussion a little differently. It really is a juggling of time committed to work related activities against time committed to family or personal activities. It actually is a problem in today's work force, for the baby boomers and earlier generations were pretty much conditioned to always put work first. This is no longer true for the generations currently entering into the work force. Promotions will be turned down, over-time refused and weekends protected, because "there is more to life than working." You simply didn't hear that from past generations! Work was always the priority.

Balance has a new meaning, and new phrases are emerging, like "work hard, play hard," or "family first." The fifties model of mom at home and dad working just isn't anymore. We're making different choices.

Finding one's balance points is just that, the process of making choices about forces that pull us in different directions. Learning how to balance will provide the foundation that allows for integration, the ultimate goal of our spiritual journey, and that will be explored a bit later. Just think of all the words we pair that require balancing: work/home, diet/exercise, play/sleep, learn/apply. And the correct "point" is unique to each person.

One of the pairings that impacts the spiritual process is that of product and process. On one of our trips to Sedona, I had a tarot reading done by a delightful woman who used the cards as a means of sharing guidance information. The lesson that was clearly shared for me was my tension between product and process. In the nicest of tones, she suggested that I needed to focus more on process and less on product. This, of course, only raised more questions. What is the process stuff? And what products am I focusing on? And what does that have to do with being spiritual?

That was well over a decade ago, and I still examine these points on a regular basis. Here's what I learned about myself that might be useful to you. I was raised to be an achiever, doing well in school, sports, music and church. I knew I was doing well, because I achieved measurable things, like good grades, starting positions, solos and leadership roles. I learned to set goals, deadlines, and measurable outcomes. When I achieved them, I felt good and was recognized as being good. Thus, the cycle of being product focused was established. You know you've arrived because a tangible product is produced or achieved. Meditation is good, so learn to do meditation, in a whole bunch of styles. Healing is good, so learn some form of therapy. Wisdom is good, so read tons of books written by the masters and be able to quote them. Physical health is good, so work out to achieve weight and fitness goals. Emotional health is good, so spend time with counselors and share your feelings. The list can be endless. The good news of being product focused is that you can measure your gains. The bad news of being product focused is that you constantly need new products.

So, I needed a little more process focus, eh? Process focus seems to be a slippery slope, for it is more dynamic and "state of being" focused, rather than tangible-results focused. In other words, it is often difficult to tell if you're accomplishing your goal! There is no finish line - you're running for the joy of running. There is no competition, no person or time to beat. Just running. Perhaps running smoothly, with an increased sense of fluidity and strength, and an ability to appreciate the environment around you while running, and yet, still just running.

So, of course, process is very important to the spiritual journey. It is not just about what you accomplish, it is your ability to integrate your "learning" and "doing" into to your state of being. The yoga master may sit for forty days without food or drink, and if that only results in being hungry and thirsty, then it's not really a big deal in the spiritual dance. The purpose of process is the state of being that one might discover, the ability and insight generated by unique conditions that make you a better person.

Probably few of us have attempted the path of the yoga masters, however many of us have gone on weekend retreats at special places with special people, and became very cosmic and communal. These were great weekends, and people did wonderful things and learned and grew. And then we went back to "reality" on Monday and could remember little of the weekend bliss by Wednesday. Great products, poor process, little integration.

Process focus demands that you answer questions such as, "How are people experiencing you?" "What is your state of being?" "What energy are you putting out?" In some ways, the only means for measuring process is discovered in the feedback from others, most of which may not be articulated or even be conscious. So, you have moments. Moments of reflection, of a brief knowing, of insight; moments of a brief comment that illuminates a key issue for you, and moments of peace and contentment.

The spiritual journey is also impacted by another set of words that I often pair together, consistency and centeredness. Unlike product and process, this pair does not reflect forces that you must balance with a sense of tension, these words rather work like a team of horses pulling a wagon, not that many of us actually have much experience with horses and wagons!

"Being centered" is a phrase I reflect upon often. It is a state of being that I experience as calm, calming, positive, grounded, enabling and a whole bunch of other positive words. It is physical, emotional, mental and spiritual. It is an alignment of being with a common focus and experience. It can also be elusive. It is the place where one can achieve balance. Okay, so words really have a difficult time in capturing this state of being, correct?

For me, being centered starts with the physical. I'm able to initiate the experience by focusing on my breathing and my third and fourth chakras (solar plexus and heart). I use sound by dropping an "ahh" into my chest, building resonance. I shift consciousness and take in my environmental stimulus without immediate response, allowing it to simply be. In addition, I consciously choose selected values and principles, most notably the flow of energy or love.

So you may ask, "I assume you are not centered in the midst of working, for you can't be doing all that and still be in the room!" The answer is, actually you can. The learning of your elements of "centeredness" requires focus and time, separate from interacting with others. However, once learned and made into a habit, you can establish that state of being as a starting point for any moment of time, and you may go back to it in a heartbeat as well. The key is the use of anchors. An anchor is a simple conscious reminder of a conditioned state of being. It could be a phrase, word, gesture, sound and/or action. For me, it is a thought and a single breath, and takes about 1.5 seconds to evoke. I make it part of my daily disciplines. I encourage you to develop your patterning of centering as well.

The second word I pair with centeredness is consistency. Consistency is doing "it" more often than not, whether that "it" is a behavior, a feeling, an attitude, or a state of being. Consistency is a discipline, an approach to one's daily routines. Most of us are very consistent in our unconscious patterns. How we get up in the morning, what we eat, how we dress, how we greet people and even how we approach our work, are all pretty consistent. However, they tend to be the consistencies of habitual patterns rather than the discipline of "applied consistency." The latter requires conscious choosing, conscious monitoring, and the conscious building of new patterns and responses. This is the "applied consistency" that aids the spiritual journey.

Part of any spiritual journey is the learning of new insights and the ability to apply those insights. We may "learn" something new in a wide variety of formats and settings, and then we face the challenge of integration and application. The pattern of applied consistency - taking the insight, and consciously looking for variances, modifications of thought and behavior, and the building of new habits and responses, is the key to our spiritual maturation. The more subtle the insight, such as with beliefs, values and principles, the more disciplined one needs to be in application. Spiritual growth occurs through the process of applied consistency. Now, match consistency with centeredness, and you're unstoppable!

There is another pair of words I wish to address as well, ebb and flow. It seems to me that part of being human is to recognize the very fluidity of our lives. Perhaps it is because we're mostly composed of water, for we surely appear to run with tides! Isn't it amazing how one can feel great, totally centered and at peace with the world, and wake up the next day on a different planet? Even in the course of a single day, our energy level and mood may swing from one compass point to another. This can be very frustrating and discouraging, especially as one attempts to honor the spiritual journey. One moment you're "one with the universe," and the next you're "hitting every red light!" This is the ebb and flow of life.

My observation is that ebb and flow happens, so don't get too excited about it. Just allow it to happen, observe it, notice the change in your state of being, avoid fighting or negative pulls, and calmly re-adjust. It is also important to note that ebbs and flows can run for much longer than an hour or a day or a week or a month. Some run for years, and require some serious adjustment! Ebbs and flows are indicators of both environmental conditions and internal choices, and both can be conscious or unconscious, within or outside our control or influence. If they're gentle patterns, then they're probably no big deal. But if they become big spikes, then it is time for conscious monitoring and action, for something is up. The primary tool one has to use is that of the "observer," and that will be the subject of the next chapter.

Ultimately, one is looking for a pretty steady flow of universal energy on the spiritual journey. This flow goes by many names, and my favorite is love. Allowing yourself to live in a state of love is allowing the energy of the universe to flow through you, positively impacting both you and all those you encounter. It doesn't have to be a big thing, just a simple state of being that others find calming and pleasant to be around, like greeting folks with a smile and assumption of positive intent. It can also be powerful, acting as an agent of healing and advocacy. The key is the flow, recognizing that the energy is flowing through you, not of you. Love is a state of being.

Balance is the key, the key between product and process, consistency and centeredness, and ebb and flow. Balance is maintaining appropriate focus and integration of key factors, such as reflected by the above pairings. All are important, all require attention, balance is the maintenance of all balls in the air. All of these words are important and may propel you in your journey. Focusing only on one element tends to make you travel in big circles, for straight flight is difficult with only one strong wing.

developing the observer

Do you ever notice that when you do something you think is really stupid, a little voice goes off in your head, saying, "That was a bonehead move!" Or, in the middle of a major rant, some part of you goes, "Wow, you're really excited!" Ever wonder who's talking inside your head?

One of the most important tools that each of us possess is that of the observer. The observer is that piece of ourselves that apparently is linked with being conscious, with being self-aware. It is the part of us that is paying attention to what we think, say, do, feel, and reflect. It is like our own personal hall monitor. Generally, it's the part that holds up the other side of our internal dialog.

Unfortunately, most of us do not realize the full potential of this wonderful tool. If anything, we often find it to be an irritant, something that nags us, forcing us to look at dynamics and aspects of life that we'd just as soon let go. For example, since I believe every emotional state is a choice, when I get mad and I'm huffing about, that voice goes off asking me, "So just how long do you intend to keep this up?" Unfortunately for me, my wife asks me the same question, so I might just respond, "For about three more hours!" And then I'm conscious of my emotional state and can no longer be in that exact emotional state, so the "mad" fades away.

The observer does just that, observe. It works both externally and internally. It is the part that is witness to the words and actions of others, even as we are participating in that very action. It is my belief that the development of the observer is the critical key to all counseling techniques and disciplines, and is also central to the spiritual journey.

Remember the discussion on intent/thought/word/deed/ reflection? In order to have an alignment of self, in order to know if one has properly set one's intention, one must be able to accurately monitor the results. If you set an intention of being a positive, helpful person, and then think mean thoughts, say rude and hurtful things and behave generally in an unfriendly manner, it would be less than helpful to say to yourself, "I'm being the person I intended to be." One would suspect you're not reading the data properly. In reading the data properly, we generally use a number of sources, including the response of others, the actual words used, the actual actions taken, and our own internal responses. However, they are all only as good as the observer. If the observed data is bad, then probably you're not listening to your observer. Instead, you may be listening to another aspect of yourself that is filtering the data through a particular historical pattern. I'll talk more about that in a minute.

The observer is the neutral party inside you. When I'm doing training with folks, I have them do this exercise, so do it in your imagination and it will still work. Sitting in teams of three, form a triangle with positions A, B and C. Everyone gets to do all three positions. Now, the person in position A, tell only the person in position B what you believe the best vacation spot in the world to be, and what makes it the best. Position B person, your job is to actively listen. You may actively listen with gestures, sounds and clarifying questions. The only thing you can't do is the normal sharing of your opinion as to the best vacation spot. Position C is to observe and only observe, and does not get to interact at all in the discussion. Position C is to monitor what is said, how it is said, and what non-verbal clues are provided for both Positions A and B. Ready? GO! After a few minutes, then everyone takes a moment to reflect on their experience silently. Then we rotate positions and do it again. After everyone has done the exercise, as you have just done, then we do a group debrief. Generally, the key lessons include that Position A is the owner of the story, and therefore the most animated and emotionally involved in the event. Position B is engaged, though less emotionally involved unless A is a really good storyteller, for it is not their story. Position C is the least involved, often feels like being in a "step back" position, and is full of actual observations of what really took place between A and B. Position C often observes the dynamics, gestures and tonality that neither A or B was consciously aware of exhibiting. Now, here is the kicker – all three of these positions are aspects of ourselves in normal human interaction. We do them all, and we do them simultaneously.

Think about the exercise and the positions. If I change the subject from your favorite vacation experience, a positive event, to your worst customer service experience, boy, do the dynamics shift. I did this in a workshop once, and it took me an hour to get the folks in a good space again! Even in an exercise, people own Position A, and the telling of their story returns them to that emotional memory/reality. They got mad again, and the folks in Position B got irritated because they had to receive A's mad. And that's how it works in real time. We share our story, someone listens, everyone responds. If we don't like being yelled at, we yell back, sometimes politely and sometimes in kind. I suggest that at that moment we've two people both in Position A, and no one is really listening anymore. So how do we break the vicious cycle? Position C. The neutral one, the least emotionally involved one, the observer.

Since we are all three, in real time, what happens is two people shifting between Positions A and B, sometimes sharing or telling the story, and sometimes listening and responding. Regardless of whether we're in position A or B, from both we shift back and forth to C. We do this so fast and unconsciously that it appears to be simultaneous, or we think that the C role is actually part of the A or B roles. But it isn't, it is a separate and distinct aspect of our being, the observer.

For most people, the observer exists as part of the automatic program, doing its job, providing its data, assisting us in our interaction with others and the world. It functions as part of our vast unconscious database of experience that is the basis of our unconscious habits and filters, of what we consider to be "normal." But it can be more.

I said that the observer is the key to all counseling techniques. Counseling is the process of assisting someone in discovering something about themselves that they might find useful in changing something about themselves. We call it many things, and yet, the bottom line is the same, figure out what isn't working, and fix it. Good counselors know that they can't fix anything, only the person can. So, for counselors, it's all about influence, and the ability to guide and assist, create options and generate good plans. I've taken training in a number of counseling disciplines and have found positive techniques that are applicable in all of them. No one system provides the answer for all situations in my mind, but the composite provides a useful toolbox. The key to all of them is the effective use of the observer. What generally makes a good counselor is a really good observer who tracks on the correct clues and uses the most appropriate methods for assisting the other person in their own healing. Good counselors have consciously developed their observer, honing its skills and capabilities.

Now, this is very important. We are all counselors. We just use different labels, like spouse, friend, mother, father, sister, brother, bartender, neighbor, fellow passenger on the plane or any other context in which we actively listen, share and interact with another human being, if only for a brief moment. Exercising the observer in a conscious manner is very useful to all of us.

The observer is critical to finding success on your spiritual journey. We all own our own lives, we set up the game plan, we play the game, and we evaluate how we did. Lessons are learned; new ones are generated. How well we do during the game is based primarily on how effectively we use our observer.

Spiritual journeys are very personal by definition. I believe they are the most intimate expression of personal growth and maturation that can ultimately be defined and assessed only by oneself. However, an individual's journey may be very noticeable, a life of service or devotion that is played out in very public settings. Just think of Mother Theresa, living a life of complete devotion and service and inviting the entire world to participate in her personal journey. Most of us think of her as a saint, and yet her real spiritual evaluation is her's alone.

I suspect she did well, but who am I to judge? Only she can assess her intention and results, only she can evaluate her life plan. Good deeds do not, by definition, mean success on the spiritual journey, they may just be good deeds. Of course, when in doubt, go with the good deeds!

The observer works both externally and internally. The observer is our prime mode of figuring out what's going on around us, and it is our prime mode for figuring out what's going on within us. Think of it as a spotlight that you direct in the dark, bringing illumination in the middle of the night. There is the unknown, and then there is light and you know the source of the noise. Now, shine the spotlight on the workings of your mind, emotions, actions and being. Who goes there? What are they doing? What are the drivers?

You may have noticed I just said "they" in referring to oneself as though the self were plural. One model that I find useful is Roberto Assagioli's *Pschosynthesis*. The reason I like this psychological map is that it is complex, and recognizes the spiritual dimension of human existence as well as the emotional and physical. This map recognizes that each of us is composed of a number of subsets, called sub-personalities. Each of these sub-personalities reflects distinct characteristics that generate a profile that becomes the filter through which others experience us. Each sub-personality has its own language, behaviors and rules of engagement. For example, in my life several sub-personalities have included the jock, the graduate student, the warehouse worker, the husband, the minister and the beaten up junior high kid. Some have been useful and positive, others have been injured and required some healing. Some propel and some inhibit. I will tell you that it gets tricky if you get them mixed up in their respective environments, like when my warehouse guy came out while doing church work. Wow, the language mix just wasn't good!

In assisting others, a common comment I hear is, "I guess that's just who I am." And my reply is always two-fold, "That is your choice, "and "Just which 'I' is speaking?" So, this often generates confusion when you ask someone, "Who said that?" The answer being, "I did." But when the sub-personality model is applied, you realize that "I" is a complex set of subs, and a consistent, singular "I" is rare, if possible at all. Being able to identify the sub means being able to heal/modify/enhance that aspect of self much more easily than not. Roberto's model is one of identifying, healing, and allowing subs to mature (we get stuck), blending and merging, into a synthesis, a whole that is aligned with the Soul. I like it. And guess what, the key to this entire process is the ability to effectively observe. In fact, one of the common subs is the guide or wise man or woman that each of us has, who plays a critical role in the interaction and modification of other subs. Sounds like the observer to me!

So how does one develop the observer? Do you need to take training in various psychological programs? Does reading help a lot? Do you need to find a guru?

Well, yes to all options, and if one or more fits for you, go for it. There is another way that all of us have available to use if we choose. And that is to simply practice and practice and practice. The way we exercise our observer, making it more conscious and integrated into our practices, is to answer these two questions. *Endlessly.*

1. What is going on with this person?

2. What do I observe, hear or feel that I may use?

All counseling techniques are answering one of these two questions. You can find the answers for yourself by practicing them endlessly. I've been doing them for decades now, and every day I learn something new about myself or someone else. It works.

Allow me to break them down a bit. Question number 1 asks, "What is going on with this person?" Now for me, this person is either external (another person) or internal (some sub-personality of mine). The critical element in asking the question is from what place do I answer it? The only possibility is the observer, good old Position C. Hence, by merely asking myself the question, I am able to consciously put myself in Position C, potentially pulling myself out of the emotional involvement of either Position A or B, if only for a micro-second. And suddenly, a world of data is made available to me, new dynamics or clues that my emotions or sub-personality was masking from my attention. It automatically puts me in that step-back position that is so useful in moving forward. It provides me the opportunity for perspective and to generate options. So, ask again, and again.

While asking this question and following the responses, guard against a very "American" response, to immediately judge. Simply resist the judgment and stay with the observation. Someone who is clearly upset and yelling, we immediately tend to judge as angry and typically start addressing the cause of their anger. That may be an accurate analysis, yet the corrective action may actually be down the road a bit. So, start with the observed, which takes us to question number two.

Number 2 asks a two-part question, "What do I observe" and "that I may use?" What do I observe is in the immediate now, the in-your-face reality of that exact moment. Back to my example, if a person is yelling at you, what you observe is the volume of his/her voice, the harsh language being used (I didn't even know he/she knew my mother), the red face and the

bulging veins. Yes, the person is probably angry for some reason, but that is a judgment not quite useful yet. Deal with the
directly observable first, and do so by finishing the question
"that I may use." This opens up the proactive consideration of
options, as opposed to the reactive response of whatever sub-
personality is currently in play. Now, mind you, the options list
may be short and considered in micro-seconds, but you can
speed time up as needed. This is particularly true if the best
option is "run!" However, we generally stay, so other options
are good to consider. Once, when a person was screaming at
me, I replied in a firm, neutral voice, "You're yelling at me."
He sputtered, started yelling again, to which I replied, "You're
still yelling at me." This time the sputtering quickly tapered off.
Remember, one cannot be in an emotional state, become conscious of that state and remain in that same, exact state. Upon
giving up his rage, issues could then be dealt with, and not
before. Thus, a dramatic illustration of the use of the questions!

A better example is hanging out in the grocery store line, and
observing a badge on the check-out clerk of a young girl in a
cheer leading outfit on it, and inquiring with good tonality,
"You know this cheerleader?" I then received the full story of
a dedicated daughter, the expense and time commitments of
cheerleading, and the heartbreaks and joys it brings. This was
the result of practicing the questions, and being in presence
with good intent. And my wife asks why everyone working in
our local Safeway seems to know me? They are my friends,
and I never stop practicing.

Technique is useful, whether from counseling disciplines or
meditation or group work or whatever. All technique makes
you more proficient at asking the questions, and yet, answering the questions is the primary basis for positive impact.
Answering the questions develops the observer, and the

observer is your personal key to growth in any dimension - physical, mental, emotional or spiritual. Movement happens, and it happens best with good information and data. Your observer can provide you with the clues you need to become the person you choose to be.

humor/laughter/perspective

I recently had a manager who worked in an organization where I was doing some consulting say, "I know when you're in the building, for I hear your laugh, and I smile."

One of the aspects of life in the Silicon Valley is that people have simply become too serious about everything. Work hard, play hard. The problem is that the emphasis has shifted to the "hard" part. Everything tends to be hard. Work is serious, and requires a serious demeanor, and a serious attitude. Calvin would be proud.

The first time I have a meeting in an organization, one of the big indicators I focus on is the noise level. I note how loud and what type of noise is being generated. Then I monitor the people dynamic, particularly how much non-verbal contact is made and if smiles and laughter exist. Clues such as these point to the nature and quality of the organization's culture.

When the clues include silence, no smiles or eye contact, the organization is inevitably dealing with morale and trust issues.

Humor has fallen on tough times in the work place. Now, this is good in that for a great number of organizations, the humor was inappropriate, whether it was jokes that were racist or sexist, or practical jokes that weren't. Political correctness did its job, and much of that humor has been removed, as it should be. However, somehow we threw the baby out with the bath water. Appropriate humor is healthy, and makes for a happier environment, which according to most productivity studies is a major force in increased productivity. And doesn't smiling require less muscle work than frowning?

I like laughing, chuckling and smiling real loud. Real stuff, no phony or nervous or polite stuff, just real, genuine responses to whatever is going on. It makes me more human. And it appears to help others be more human as well. I mean, we're not machines, we're not perfect, life happens. We need some perspective.

Appropriate humor is ultimately the ability to have perspective in any given moment, to allow ourselves to respond in genuine ways and not become too stressed. Appropriate humor is the Bill Cosby style that allows one to relate, be a part of the normal dance of humans, to make mistakes and continue. It is often the "icing" that allows difficult issues to be raised and successfully addressed.

My wife has often observed that I get away with saying the rudest things to folks, and yet they don't take offense and generally will do something with whatever I've said. For me, it's a simple recipe for success. I enter the interaction with positive intent, for I am genuinely interested in the person and willing to assist to the degree requested. Please note, all the verbs and adjectives in that sentence are very important. Then, I share only that which is easily observable, and remember that love is more important than truth. Add doing it with positive non-verbals and some genuine humor. It is amazing what people will accept when the response is genuine, true and served with a strong dose of humanity and laughter. It's hard to get mad when you're smiling and laughing. The very humanity of the dynamic leads to acceptance of the person, even when a particular behavior or action is being confronted. Again, no phony stuff, and certainly, not every situation is appropriate for humor, though equally not every situation is appropriate for gravity. We really can lighten up.

Real humor isn't jokes, because jokes are usually based on someone being a loser. I like good jokes and enjoy talented comedians, though if you carefully listen, you will notice that someone is typically the "butt" of the joke. And we all laugh, largely because it isn't us, and when we are, it is a test. Real humor is being able to laugh or smile in the moment, based upon the immediate response to the observable. Real humor is often conveyed in the sound in which we wrap the words, not the actual words used.

In face-to-face communication, 7% of the message is the actual words we use, 38% is the sound and 55% is the non-verbals. Now sound includes pace, pitch, tone, intonation and resonance, while the non-verbal is far more than body movement, with the majority of clues happening in the face. But think about these numbers and the proven importance of the actual words we use, and then realize that 93% of the message is not the words! When I'm doing training in this stuff, I challenge every group to give me a short phrase, and I will be able to change its meaning without changing a word. I've yet to lose.

Real humor is generally conveyed in the 93%. It is the multi-level message of acceptance, forgiveness and/or humanness that is attached to whatever your specific content might be. It becomes the medium that allows someone to accept and truly hear what might be a bitter pill. Again, it's not applicable in every situation, and yet I fear that we don't apply it nearly enough.

And there is a reason for that non-application. We've lost perspective.

Perspective exists at multiple levels, so allow me to address just a few, and then you add your own. Let's start with work. I am so unfavorably impressed with the increased number of articles reporting on how attached we've become to work. We must do work all the time, and we must be connected all the time. Cell phones, wireless laptops, emails and 24/7 availability are becoming the norm. Going on vacation requires taking your electronic toys and checking in, and providing a back-up list of numbers for urgent contact. No, I say, vacation means not being available and not being present, it's doing something else. And yet, too many of us believe that "work" will simply crash and burn without our immediate and constant attention. Equally to blame is the pattern of many who work long days, come home and briefly eat and greet, and return to work on the bed or at the home office. So, what is it? Too much work? Not enough resources? Fear of being replaced? Addiction?

I know these issues, for I was once a clear work-a-holic. If these words ring a bell for you, please consider the following. Should you get hit by a bus tomorrow, you will be mourned and replaced, and perhaps not in that order. You are not irreplaceable; unique, yes, irreplaceable, no. And consider, when you're life is nearing its end, will you be glad that you worked all those weekends? And finally, is this how you want/choose to spend your existence? If your answer is yes, fine, but if not, then get some perspective.

Another critical place for perspective is in dealing with other human beings. It's been quite a while since we've had reports of folks walking on water, so unless you're one who can, perhaps remembering to be human is good. For me, to be human is to recognize our complexity, and to remember that humans make mistakes. So why do we expect perfection? Are we not human? Yet we do expect perfection. We expect it of others and we expect it of ourselves, and we beat ourselves and others up when it doesn't happen. Now, consistency is one of my major principles, and I work hard at being highly consistent relative to things I care about, but perfection? It simply doesn't appear to be part of the human make-up. Be human, allow yourself to make mistakes. We learn from mistakes. If we can figure out perfection, then a whole bunch of ice skaters are going to be happy, and we'll be bored watching the Olympics.

It is often the case that we are most hard on those closest to us. Yet if you just take a second, back up one step, that simply doesn't make sense. Doesn't it make more sense that those closest to us should get the most support, love and space to be human? Yet we don't. Too close, perhaps? Or have we simply lost perspective?

And finally, any spiritual work demands perspective. What is your real nature? What is the true reality? Is this world really illusion, and what might that mean? Are you a soul temporarily in a body, or a body that may have a soul?

I'm not aware of any spiritual discipline that doesn't demand a new orientation and understanding of the nature of reality.

Priorities often need to be shifted, values and principles aligned, and proper perspective maintained. We need to live life fully, not timidly, and we need to act upon our beliefs. But remember, no one knows. Choose, and act upon those choices, being consistent in who you are, but keep some perspective. In Richard Bach's *Illusions*, he has the character referring to the 'Messiah's Handbook' for truth and guidance, and the last entry is, "Everything in this book may be wrong." Perspective is everything.

It is understanding the true nature of our world. Today, physicists and mystics are reaching the same conclusions. There is more space in solid matter than matter, and solid is actually moving at the particle level. And we are in fact all one, composed of the same elements, organized in more similar than dissimilar ways. We are present in this form for a relatively short period of time, and then we mix into other forms and shapes. The elements are constant; we are not.

So, what are we? Ah, now that is the big choice we each get to make. Based upon our choice, each of us organizes our individual lives, while interacting with others who are busy doing the same thing.

Interesting, the Byrds' "Turn, Turn, Turn" just came up on my stereo. Appropriate, yes? Perspective is essential for balance, centeredness and spiritual maturation. And don't forget, humor is a big key, allow yourself to laugh and smile, and see where it takes you.

comparative mind/be here now

My buddy Paul is fond of saying, "Comparison is the thief of joy." Now that's a thought worth rolling around the backside of your mind.

It implies that joy is a good state of being, and there is a dynamic that is capable of diminishing that state. Joy is one of those words that are not used very often these days, and yet it becomes very useful when considering one's state of being. Joy has that feel of something more substantial, a state that is more long-term than fleeting, the potential for being a constant. While happy has that short-term ring to it, joy is going to hang around.

From a more spiritual perspective, joy echoes a sense of calm that reflects a profound connection with the universe. Joy describes our state of being as one becomes immersed in watching the sun set over the Golden Gate Bridge, or when sitting in a forest and having the wind whisper secrets in your ear. Joy is being comfortable in your own skin, content with your life, secure in your sense of identity. Joy is expressed as subtle yet profound energy radiating outward from your center and offering a touch-less hug to all who pass within its radiance.

Joy is a good thing, so what a pity to lose it. Unfortunately, losing touch with joy is easy to do in our culture, and one of the easiest means is the comparative mind. One of the clear American cultural values is competition, with the goal of being the winner. No one remembers who came in second place, let alone remember who was even in the race. I don't think competition is bad, though it's good to know its limitations. Competition forces us into a constant state of comparison, measuring our stuff against someone else's stuff. Jill, my wife, made this brilliant comment relative to a young friend of ours who plays basketball. "She enjoys playing basketball, but isn't that competitive about it." Competition is the drive that forces us to rank the relative skill and abilities of individuals, making some winners and some losers. It applies to teams, organizations and countries. As a culture, we fully embrace competition, so we compare everything: houses, income, physical appearances, clothing, cars, work, positions, children, spouses, religions, churches, teams and sleep. There simply is no end, for anything we have we will compare to someone else's. Guess we're out of luck when it comes to having joy. Unless.

Unless what? We'd have to give up the comparative mind. It is possible, and perhaps one can still be competitive in the midst of its absence. The comparative mind is fully *attached* to the elements that it is comparing. What if you allowed the comparison to be a piece of data, useful in determining performance levels or thresholds for limited participation activities, such as team sports? It would allow for competition, and wouldn't demand the emotional element of judgment. What if the element being compared is not a part of your identity? Then, you are doing or not doing, making the cut or not, and not, by definition, becoming a loser. Who you are is grounded in some other awareness that cannot be touched by the specific element under review. The key is the attachment to what is being measured. So, give up the attachment, and the power of the comparison is removed, allowing joy to still be present.

Sounds good, but tough to do, and almost impossible when still an adolescent. Gad, everything has to be checked with your peers, and the comparative mind is the norm. Still, it is possible to escape adolescence, and it is possible to choose an alternative way of interacting with your environment that doesn't demand the comparative mind. The spiritual journey generally calls us to embrace our commonality and oneness with each other and our environment. Focusing on what we hold in common and appreciating the wonderful variety of expression and ability can limit the impact of comparison, and allow joy to exist. By the way, being in a spiritual community does not automatically free you from the trap of comparison. There is just as much potential melodrama there as any other place, and if expanded, leads to the tribal based warfare we are experiencing throughout the world today. It strictly depends upon your choices and how you want to interact. As an experiment, for the next couple of days, attempt to simply be observant of the number of times you find yourself comparing yourself to someone else in thought, word or deed. You don't have to act on that observation, and withhold judgment of yourself of the other person, simply observe the pattern. It is amazingly common to all of us.

One of the subtler comparisons is that of the past and the future, not allowing us to be present in the "now." Ram Dass wrote a book entitled *Be Here Now*, that has a significant six-ties feel to it, yet still speaks to a spiritual truth captured in its title. My observation is that many of us have a great difficulty with being in the present, in the now. Having made this observation for myself a couple of decades ago, I've been working on it ever since. It is really challenging. For example, you're a parent and have come home from a busy day at work and you're feeding your child, and realize you've not heard a word of their earnest explanation of the nature of bugs! Or, how often have we heard someone talking about their life, and the singular focus is on retirement? And how far off is that?

I listened to a motivational speaker years ago whose primary message was that most of us spend our adult lives either attempting to recreate the glory of our high school years or attempting to live them down. Either way, our current lives and self-images are more likely to reflect our high school time than our current realities. Think about it. Do you think of yourself as thin or heavy? What is the truth now? I was always a skinny kid, and I'm often surprised that I now take up as much space as my 6 foot, 220 pounds frame does. Go figure. Do you know someone who was a "star" in high school? Are they still talking about the events of high school as if they just hap-pened? Do they compare their life today to their life then? That's living in the past. There clearly is a fair amount of truth in that speaker's model. We all carry ghosts of who we once were, and they influence us today.

Certain therapy models and criminal justice rulings indicate that our past experiences are justifiable bases for current behaviors, attitudes and actions. I'm not minimizing the impact of the past, however I believe I own my choices — all of them, past and current and future. When I'm working with someone who offers up the past as a reason for their current status, my primary response is, "Make new choices." Though it may be difficult, and require therapy and constant vigilance, every one of us has the opportunity and responsibility to live in the now. Regardless of the past, choose your "now." Rebuild the old habits, including behaviors, attitudes and self-image. Build new habits, form new disciplines, create new patterns of life.

The future can be as big a trap as the past. Do you know anyone who is living for their kid's graduation? The next promotion? Not getting married until the house is purchased and a certain level of income is attained? We all have plans, and it is good to have plans, and life is what is happening now. I'm not arguing for a "do whatever you want, as you want, when you want," kind of thing. I'm arguing for chosen state of being.

Think about what is going on right now around you. Be aware of what forces you are dealing with and in what manner. Realize what you are doing, right now. Realize who you are being, right now. Are you doing and being who you choose to be? Or, are you waiting for later?

To whatever degree your answer is waiting, you are not living in the present. So, make a sign, big or small, and place it wherever you'll run into it on regular basis that says, "Be Here Now." Go, Ram Dass.

As you practice being here now, you may notice subtle shifts in your response to the world. Your attention may become more focused. One of my heroes is Lazarus Long, from Robert Heinlein's *Time Enough for Love*. One of Lazarus' characteristics is the ability to focus all of his attention on a single subject or person. Very cool. I've tried to practice that art, and it is amazing what it can accomplish. It requires being in the now, with all the past and future available, but not intruding.

Being in the now allows you be present with another human being without comparison. I've noticed that I can actually listen, be attentive and be focused on their story without the pressure of response, matching stories or some quick return. This is further supported by my belief that all knowledge is available to me as I need, so I don't need to be thinking about something else while the other is talking. I can simply listen, observe and be present. Try it - it has positive impact and benefits.

Being in the now allows for joy to be a constant. It allows you to be comfortable with yourself, and that allows others to be comfortable in your presence. It allows for human moments, genuine smiles and laughter, as well as tears and hugs.

Practice. Be here now. Be. Fun.

discipline revisited

Discipline is critical to the spiritual journey. However, the word discipline has typically become associated with little that has to do with the spiritual journey of today.

Consider this phrase, "Spare the rod and spoil the child." I bet most people believe it is a line from the Bible, as it certainly has become a part of Western society's values. And it has been used as a justification for beating kids. Wrong on both counts, it is not in the Bible, and beating kids do not make them better. Unfortunately, this type of thinking is such a part of Western enculturation, that it becomes difficult to use the word discipline. For most of us, the word itself has become solely associated with corporeal punishment. There are other meanings that are more significant.

I'm not sure how Webster defines discipline, but the definition I'm advocating is "the systemic incorporation of specific patterns of thought and behavior that reflect a chosen set of beliefs, values and principles."

Spiritual enlightenment doesn't "just happen" today as far as I can tell. I wish it did! And if the magic answer was a well to drink from or a mountain to climb or a person to touch, I'd be there! But I don't think that is the main option for those of us interested in focusing on our spiritual enhancement. No, Earth School is about making choices and exercising options. If what we've chosen to do this round is to focus on our spiritual growth, then we enter into a slightly different process. Let's see if we can break down some of the big steps.

As discussed in an earlier chapter, the first step is to lay out the basic parameters before entering the Earth School. By this, I mean we select the primary goals for this round of existence, based upon the current needs of the soul's maturation, and in consultation with our team. Next, we select the culture, family, race and gender that makes the most sense relative to the big goals and other specific objectives. Then, we enter the game as newborns, and quickly begin to forget. I suspect that is essential for we need to avoid being captured by past memories, and the essence of the soul's growth is found in the very dynamic of making choices.

Second, we begin the Earth School dance. We learn the rules of family and culture, we pick up a language or two, we learn how to operate the body and the accompanying emotional and mental processes. We become conditioned, and habits are developed that we don't consciously choose, and we believe they are a natural, genetic part of who we are. Sometime along the way, we start making smaller decisions on our own, using our own matrix of ideas and understanding about who we are and how the world works. When this happens is a big variable as far as I can tell. I had a life reading

done once that indicated I started making independent choices around the age of 7, which my mother agrees with, though
she describes it as me being a little hellion.

Third, we start making mega-choices. These are the biggies,
the ones that we organize our lives around. We start examining belief systems, value sets and guiding principles. We look
at the ones we inherited, and start the acceptance, rejection,
and/or modification process. This isn't a one-time exercise for
most of us, rather a continual process that is marked by key
high points of clarity and consciousness, followed by neutral
zones and plateaus. We might describe it as one-step forward, two steps back and three steps side-ways. Interestingly,
one of the best descriptions of mastery I've read described it
as a series of staircase-like steps, characterized by periods of
chaotic change and development, followed by an establishing
plateau. In this manner, even our mega-choices are subject to
an evolutionary process of understanding and integration.

Fourth, we make the mini-choices that support our mega-choices. This is where discipline comes in. It isn't sufficient to make
a mega-choice, such as "Love is the primary glue of the universe and the guiding force of my life," and then walk away,
smug in the knowledge that you've become cosmic. Sorry, you
have to figure out how to apply it in every aspect of your
being, thought processes and behaviors. This is "systemic
incorporation."

Fifth, we get to do regular reviews leading up to the big
review. This process of reflection may be approached in a
structured manner, or it may appear to simply "happen."
At irregular moments, we have the opportunity to check the
pulse of our lives, to see if the mega-choices still make sense,
and to do some course corrections as needed. Hopefully,
we avoid the trap of constantly changing life directions in

radically different directions, it would simply be too confusing and you'd probably not really assist in the soul's maturation. For example, I've worked with organizations that seem to spend the majority of their time reorganizing. In fact, that appears to be their primary activity, and they are generally quite good at the process. Unfortunately, it feels a lot like moving deck chairs on the Titanic, and they generally lose track of their primary mission. Try to avoid that eddy, and stay in the stream. Because ultimately, we turn in our bodies, allow them to return to elements of the universe, and with our team, do the big review. Based upon our evaluation of this session of Earth School, we then set up the next round of the soul's maturation.

Neat little cycle, eh? I wish it only worked that smoothly. But that's what makes the game a good one. We get to make choices throughout the entire cycle, we own the entire process and the consequences of our choices. I suspect that Earth School is relatively unique in that manner, and that other dimensions offer other opportunities. I have no proof of course, and remember, no one knows. However, some of the best sci-fi writers think in a similar fashion, and that's good enough for me.

So, back to discipline, remember the definition I'm using is "the systemic incorporation of specific patterns of thought and behavior that reflect a chosen set of beliefs, values and principles." This is the "doing" of what was discussed under the chapter intent/thought/word/deed/reflection.

Intention is the major alignment of one's mega-choices into personal being. It is setting the overall tone and direction that guides the unconscious database with the proper filters and options for ongoing interaction with the stimulus of our lives, especially other people and our environment. In setting intention, it is important to use the proper programming language.

For the human unconscious, it requires using positive language that moves us forward. Negative language, such as, "I will not..." or "I will stop..." is not effective because the unconscious database knows that in order to stop doing something, one must first be doing it so that it can stop. Bad cycle. So, use positive language. "I am supportive, open and accepting," is a much better way to work on incorporating the energy of love into your daily interactions.

Discipline takes us into the details of our lives. We examine all the pieces, reviewing thought patterns, individual ideas, dreams and fantasies. Our observer is on constant alert, looking at the inward milieu of thoughts and emotions, noting how dots are being connected, or not. Reflection becomes a major tool. It is the examination of these observations, noting the source and evaluating the individual thoughts against the standards of the mega-choices. Remember, honesty at this level is an absolute rule, no fudging!

The work of the observer is never done. It must immediately and somewhat simultaneously listen to what is being formulated in the mind and what comes out of the mouth. Isn't it amazing how what is so crystal clear in our minds turns to mush when the mouth is engaged? At times, what pops out of our mouths appears to have no basis in what we were thinking. This is vital information that the observer will catch and lift up for reflection and consideration. Who said that? What is the source? What conditioned, unconscious element just raised its head? We are an endless source of new information and patterns, and all of that information may be considered as we choose to become who we choose to be.

Guess what? The pattern repeats itself as we move into deeds, actions, behaviors, non-verbal responses and energy patterns. Truly, we can learn and grow every, single day of our existence. If we choose.

Discipline is the key to moving forward in our lives. Each one of us must discover the tools and rituals that assist us in the appropriate development of our individual applications. Like the rest of life, there is not a set of correct procedures and protocols, you get to make up your own. By this, I don't mean you have to start from scratch on every item; you just have to decide which ones you want to use.

There must be a thousand forms of meditation, ranging from simple sitting to prayer to Sufi dancing. There are hundreds of psychological maps that provide analysis of mental and emotional patterns. Physical fitness offers options ranging from thumb twiddling to deep sea diving. We have all the major and minor religions of the world at our fingertips. So, with all these resources and options, remember the lessons of integration, it is probably impossible to learn everything. And even if it is, so what? Take what makes sense, and integrate it into your system of knowing and being. I ask that you remember there are a lot of options out there, so avoid becoming too judgmental about the choices others make. Sure, if their choices mean harming you, then you might consider whether to die or fight back, but truly consider your full range of choices. You, like the other person, get to fully own both choice and consequence.

For me, I try to keep it as simple as possible. I've attempted to learn and integrate from all the tools I've been exposed to and the books I've read and the people I've encountered. I've explored a variety of reflection tools, and find sitting, driving and listening to music extremely useful when consciously approached. I continue to read, both fiction and non-fiction. I pay increasing attention to my intention, both as a daily set-up and during the course of the day. I work at perspective and centeredness. My way is the way of the mind, so my tools reflect that particular path. You may well have different tools.

Common to all who choose to focus on the spiritual path are the steps of choosing, implementing and reflecting. A tight little cycle that is endless, and defined by the disciplines selected and imposed. Choose wisely.

living a God-centered life

Is it possible?

I mean, to truly follow a spiritual path in the midst of our materialistic, Western culture, is it possible? Yes, though many are loudly proclaiming that is exactly what they are doing, I have my doubts. Certainly, many of the loudest voices will probably not be pleased with the musings shared within this book.

Being of the West, I must address the God thing, and as I suggested in *the order of things* chapter, it is time to give up theism. A supernatural being who sits outside our world, occasionally intervening to either rescue or punish, is a model of the past. Many would argue that that mythological structure has been replaced by science, materialism, humanism or some mix therein. The "God is dead" thinking. I've not gone there.

My understanding of being human is that of a whole entity comprised of physical, mental, emotional and spiritual dimensions. These dimensions are closely inter-related, and one impacts another, for we are, in fact, whole. When I consider the spiritual dimension, I believe there is something that continues beyond the obvious life cycle of the physical body, and that I call the soul. Furthermore, I believe that the life cycle is really about providing an opportunity for the soul to continue its maturation and development.

Being human, we are conscious, aware beings. One of the things we are aware of is our own death. We're not clear on when or how necessarily, but we "know" it is going to happen. This awareness produces a fair amount of anxiety, and in turn produces a need for understanding and a desire for security. We generally seek answers and security relative to death within our religions. Therefore, we take our religions very seriously, and if someone has a different view, we are willing to go to war, because if they're right, we might be wrong, and then our security is destroyed. Unfortunately, no one *knows*, and no religion has absolute authority.

So, is living a God-centered life possible? I answer with a quiet *yes*.

But it is really challenging. We've certainly set up a complex obstacle course, yet that's the nature of the Earth School. I suspect that we are in the midst of a significant shift of spirit, perhaps as part of the cumulative maturation of the human spirit. One aspect of the shift is the focus on individual ownership as opposed to joining the right club. The conditions are right. We have access to the entire world's knowledge and experience, we know that life is evolutionary and continues to do so, and for many of us, survival is not the only game in town. We have the time, resources and the capacity.

My answer is a quiet yes. Now is not a time of revolution, rather a time of building new patterns of spiritual questing. Instead of following a single, historical system of faith, we have the capacity to mix and match. It is a time for creating new patterns, finding guides and resources for the moment rather than a guru for life. I am comfortable being strongly influenced by Jesus of the Bible, Buddha and his teachings, and a host of more current authors. It is mine to own, design, implement and evaluate. And there is still a place for God.

Living a God-centered life is a commitment statement of pursuing a spiritual journey as the primary focus of this life. This journey may take as many forms as there are individuals. That is a reflection of our diversity. The commonality is the recognition that we are each a spiritual being in a physical body, and the purpose of our participation in Earth School is the maturation of the soul.

Here are a couple of key focal points from my perspective.

One, we must embrace the mystery. It is actually okay to not have clearly defined answers as to the nature of the universe, God, and our place within it. It is a bit scary, and anxious folk run the risk of being governed by fear. Our challenge is to resist fear and embrace the mystery. Embracing the mystery allows you to fully participate and engage in the cycle of birth, life and death. It is knowing that you are a part of life and an expression of life without knowing all of the rules and even being able to fully comprehend its complexity. How can the finite grasp the infinite?

Living a God-centered life leads to an understanding of connectivity. Whether you get this understanding through science as sub-atomic theory or through mystic contemplation of your breath, it gets you to the same place. Connectivity is the realization that all of life is profoundly linked. Our historical patterns of separation, including our very definition of individual selves, nations, plant and animal life, and the planet itself are not necessarily how life is ultimately organized. The Hubble Telescope allows us to graphically understand that the entire universe is seriously large, complex, and moving within a relational "life flow" as well. We are seriously connected!

The vastness of our connectivity can lead to a fear-based sense of being small and insignificant, or it can lead to a sense of being part of a magnificent expression of life that certainly exceeds our capacity to fully grasp. I choose the latter. This is the mystery, and the mystery I call God. All of life, from the sub-atomic particle to the exploding super-nova to you and me becomes an expression of God. We are connected, to all of the expressions of life, to each other. *Namaste* - the God in me greets the God in you.

Choosing to embrace the mystery also means embracing the need to be fully human within the Earth School. This includes making and owning all the necessary mega and mini-choices that sustain both the individual's and the community's existence. The mystery is fully participating in the paradox of making choices upon which you run your very life, and knowing they may be meaningless or wrong. How uncomfortable is that? Not knowing is not a popular thing with us. We like to know, to be correct, to be right. Sorry, it's a mystery. Life is much more complex than we can *know*. Embrace it. It's okay, really.

Secondly, we must decide what are the primary drivers and benchmarks that we use in our individual spiritual journey. There are many that I find significant, and they're certainly scattered throughout this book. In addition, I offer these words as borrowed from Bishop John Shelby Spong, "We are called by the mystery of God to live fully, love wastefully and Be all that we can be." These are my current, favorite expressions.

To "live fully," what does that evoke for you? For me, it calls me to fully participate, to delve into all the questions that life offers, to own my choices and deal with the consequences. It requires me to consider my ethics, my relationships with other people, critters and the planet itself. It requires me to choose how people will experience me, and to pay attention to both product and process. It calls me to explore and take risks rather than be fear-based. It is to be a responsible agent of life, recognizing that I am a transient in a much larger picture, though fully empowered to learn lessons I need to feed my soul.

And "to love wastefully," don't these words feel like the warmth of the sun on a cool day or the giggle of a child snuggling into the comfort of your arms? There is tremendous freedom is these words. It immediately reminds us that love is not ours to own or hold; rather that love flows through and around us. Love is universal and we are invited to swim in its endless depths and capacity. The more we share and pass around, the more becomes available to us. It is the demand to reach out, participate in the larger community, contribute, risk, share and support. Loving wastefully is a state of being.

"To Be" is to fully realize our potential and expression of our humanity. To be is to recognize that each one of us is a unique expression of life. To assist and support others in their full development and expression of life is to enhance our own development and expression. To be is to participate in the very expression of God, the Ground of All Being, as articulated by Paul Tillich. At the spiritual level, it is the recognition of God in all of life, the creatures of life and the processes of life. At the individual level, it is the full development of mind, body, emotions and spirit. Be is a little word with a big punch.

Yes, it is possible to live a God-centered life. It is perhaps the underlining mission of human existence and the ultimate expression of the soul. It is a choice, perhaps the mega-choice of all. The ripples of this choice will fill your entire life, and will fill it with love and joy, as well as a fair amount heartache and pain. That's the nature of Earth School, and it is in session. It is up to you to decide who you want to be, and how you want to play.

I suggest — live fully, love wastefully and be completely.

reminders

Anything written faces an interesting challenge – it becomes fixed in time. The words become a concrete statement of fact, and often we treat these words as if their very existence constitutes fact. However, words only represent a particular slice of reality as understood at a particular point in time within a particular cultural framework. This applies to all written words, including this book.

I know that my understanding of the concepts shared within this book continue to evolve as my soul and being matures. I probably won't make dramatic shifts in my thinking, and yet, who knows? We all need to be open to new insights every moment of our lives. That's what earth school is all about – learning, evolving, becoming, being.

You are a spiritual being in a physical body. Allow the spirit to play, enable the soul to mature, maintain your perspective, love wastefully and fully Be.

recommended reading

The following authors and books are some of my favorites with absolutely no attempt to be inclusive. Enjoy.

Assagioli, Roberto. *Psycosynthesis*
Bach, Richard. *Illusions*
Bach, Richard. *Bridge Across Forever*
Bellah, Robert. *Beyond Belief*
Dass, Baba Ram. *Be Here Now*
Dyer, Wayne W. *Wisdom of the Ages*
Dyer, Wayne W. *There's a Spiritual Solution to Every Problem*
Fox, Matthew. *Original Blessing*
Gibran, Kahlil. *The Prophet*
Heinlein, Robert. *Stranger in a Strange Land*
Heinlein, Robert. *Time Enough for Love*
Leonard, George. *Mastery*
Leonard, George & Murphy, Michael. *The Life We Are Given*
Neihardt, John. *Black Elk Speaks*

Smith, Huston. *The World's Religions: Our Great Wisdom Traditions*

Spong, John Shelby. *Jesus for the Non-Religious*

Spong, John Shelby. *Rescuing the Bible from Fundamentalism*

Strauss, William & Howe, Neil. *The Fourth Turning*

Tillich, Paul. *The Courage to Be*

Theilhard de Chardin. *The Divine Milieu*

Theilhard de Chardin. *The Phenomenon of Man*

Williams, Paul. *Das Energi*

Zukov, Gary. *The Dancing Wu Li Masters*

about the author

Tim Dunkin began this journey in the farmland of Ohio prior to becoming a Californian. Believing in multiple careers, Tim has worked as a warehouseman, minister, gardener, counselor, manager, trainer and consultant. Tim specializes in the public and non-profit sectors, and is primarily a life coach and organizational consultant. He has a degree in Philosophy and a Masters in Divinity, plus certificates in a number of counseling and training disciplines. Most importantly, he has a wonderful wife and life partner, Jill.

For more information, go to: www.DunkinWorks.com or contact Tim at:

DunkinWorks
4959 Mise Ave.
San Jose, CA 95124